CHOOSE
JOY

BABS PLUNKETT

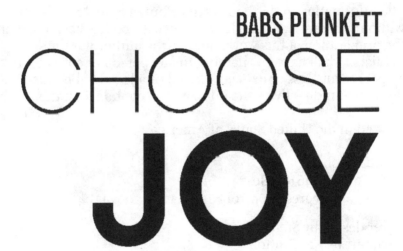

CHOOSE
JOY

Three keys
to investing your time
in retirement

Printed in the United States of America

First Edition
ISBN: 978-1-946195-80-7
Library of Congress Control Number: 2020914304

Cover design by Stefan Hartung
Cover art by Kei Gratton
Photograph by Kevin Healy Photography
Interior Book Design by Ann Aubitz
Edited by Kellie Hultgren

Published by FuzionPress
1250 E 115th Street, Burnsville, MN 55337
FuzionPress.com

TABLE OF CONTENTS

INTRODUCTION *Why Choose Joy?* |*11*

ENGAGE YOUR MIND
What Are You Doing Monday Morning? |*19*

Do Something for Others
1. Volunteering Keeps Him Going
   Grandpa Bob, 87 years |*22*
2. Award-Winning Smoke Detector Installers
   Mary and Tom, 81 years |*24*
3. Tikkun Olam, Heal the World
   Barbara, 75 years |*26*

Pursue a Passion
4. Do What You Love
   Molly, 70 years |*30*
5. If You Look for the Good, You'll Find It
   Jo, 68 years |*33*
6. Make a Plan, Live It, Revise As Needed
   Simin, 69 years |*36*

Get Creative
7. Music in the Key of Life
   Bob, 84 years |*40*
8. Tools for Living
   Sharon, 76 years |*43*
9. World Music Radio DJ
   Marta, 78 years |*46*

Unretire
    10. Law School at Age 56
        Gerry, 79 years |50
    11. The Fun of the Sale
        Bob and Mary, 88 years and 86 years |53
    12. "Failed" Retirement
        Eileen, 87 years |56

Try Something New
    13. No Limits when You Set Them Yourself
        Robin C., 82 years |60
    14. Do, Explore, Volunteer
        Larry, 62 years |63
    15. Aging Well Is a Decision You Make
        Stan R., 84 years |65

MOVE YOUR BODY
How Do You Want to Stay in Motion? |67

Move for the Joy of It
    16. Act III Adventures
        Robin D., 65 years |70
    17. Dancing into a Second Career
        Richard, 82 years |72
    18. Exercise Body and Spirit
        Peter, 92 years |74

Get Your Steps in While Giving
    19. A Week in Action
        Dorothy and Gordon, 90 years and
        93 years |78
    20. Buckthorn Removal Project
        Jim N., 72 years |80
    21. Faith on the Move
        Jim and Norma, 80 years and 70 years |82

Moving with Health Limitations
22. Time My Race with a Calendar
    Carter, 70 years |86
23. Dog Park for Fitness and Friendship
    Bill and Anne, 90 years and 56 years |88
24. Diabetes and a Song
    Audrey, 76 years |90

Get Outside
25. Woodburning Stove Workout
    Don, 76 years |94
26. Wag More, Bark Less
    Barry, 63 years |96
27. Healing in the Garden
    Winnie, 73 years |98

Untraditional Travel
28. Wilderness Guide to Peace and Friendship
    Kath, 67 years |102
29. Faith-Fueled Travel
    Sally and Elgin, 77 years |105
30. Road Tripping for Adventure and Antiques
    Dave, 76 years |109

CONNECT WITH OTHERS
Who You Gonna Call? |111

Won't You Be My Neighbor?
31. Neighbors, Friends, and Hockey Lovers
    Warren and Logan, 77 years and 7 years |116
32. Cell Phone Connection
    Lois, 100 years |118
33. If You Scoop It, They Will Come
    Norma and Jim, 70 years and 80 years |121

Grandparenting

34. Cousins' Camp
   Jane and Odin, 77 years |124
35. Just Show Up
   Jim S., 83 years |126
36. Pizza with a Side of Love
   Joy, 80 years |128

Create Bonds through Service

37. Cuban Connections
   Doris, 65 years |132
38. Finding a Friendship Match
   Kate, 67 years |134
39. One Cause, Different Roles
   Connie and Jack, 79 years |136

Join a Club or Create a Group

40. Master Club Member
   Joan, 83 years |140
41. Friendly Philosophers Group
   Gib, 68 years |142
42. Zen of Photography
   Susan, 65 years |145

Healing and Love

43. Gentle Love and Healing
   Mary, 67 years |148
44. In Sickness and in Health
   William, 77 years |150
45. Friendship and Love
   Farah and Jen, 97 years and 56 years |153

PUT IT ALL TOGETHER
Would You Like to Take the Combo? |155

Combining Mind, Body, and Relationships
    46. Cautionary Tales to Joy
        David, 73 years |158
    47. Cancer Inspired a New Path
        Betty, 72 years |161
    48. Passions That Work with Your
        Changing Body
        John, 68 years |164
    49. Pink Slip Leads to Joy and Connection
        Claire, 60 years |167
    50. Get off Your Butt!
        Stan M., 85 years |170

CONCLUSION *Are You Ready to Choose Joy?* |173

INTRODUCTION

Why Choose Joy?

*People decide, "Oh, I'm getting old, my life is over." Then they just
recline into a rocking chair and rot away. You don't have to do that!*
—*Lois, 100 years*

My grandma was the most unhappy person I've
ever met. She moved in with us when I was
thirteen years old, and the weight of her presence made a lifelong impression on me. Every day she
would perch in the kitchen, wearing a dress, high heels,
and a scowl. When I asked her about her life and her
interests, she often answered, "I don't know why God
keeps me alive. I'd rather be dead." This sad and alarming
statement made me wonder: was I genetically destined to
be unhappy, or could I choose?

For the next four decades I paid attention to people
who chose joy. I met many inspiring people—teachers,
neighbors, family members, and coworkers—and when it
felt right, I inquired about their lives and their choices.
Had they always been that way? Were they upbeat as kids,
or did they decide to be positive? Each person named a
specific time in their life when they made up their mind to
change their attitude and live better. Amazed, I felt

genuine relief upon learning that we're not destined to slide into crabbiness. Aging well is a choice. We can choose joy.

Writing this book has felt like finding a key piece to a puzzle I've been trying to solve throughout my life. For one ten-year stretch of my career I oversaw market research used to launch a music program for adults fifty-five and older at a prominent community music school in my home city, Minneapolis. The research included focus groups of older adults talking about the role of creativity and fulfillment in their lives through music and other means. Over and over they used the word *joy* to describe what they were searching for—not fleeting *happiness*, but *joy*, which seemed deeper and longer lasting. I earned certifications as a life coach and a professional retirement coach to better understand how exactly you choose joy. Working with clients who were "seeking joy and purpose" further ignited my passion and inspired me to live more joyfully too. It's one thing to say joy is a goal. To take action and live it is profound and energizing.

The sudden inspiration for this project surprised me. All my life I've been a timeline, action-plan, checklist kind of gal. I write plans for everything in my life. But this project arrived differently. There was no plan. I just woke one spring morning (March 1, 2018, to be exact) with a fiery passion to collect stories about people aging with joy and purpose. This joyful aging project came to me with no game plan, just an urgency to get going. Within two weeks I had interviewed the first fifteen people. By summer I'd spoken with about fifty people. With no plan for how I would use the stories, I just followed the thread of joy.

To find my interview subjects, I put a call out on social media for referrals to older adults living with joy and engagement. My online network is fairly broad. I'm from a large Irish Catholic family spread along both coasts and throughout the Midwest. I grew up in Michigan and went to college in Minnesota, where I currently live. Early in my career I traveled and worked throughout the United States, Canada, Europe, and China for an international service organization, working with hundreds of college-age students from fifteen countries, and stayed in touch with hundreds of people throughout the world. From these contacts I received a flood of recommendations. I focused my interviews on people in the United States because I assumed I would share the stories here and wanted them to be as relatable as possible. I interviewed people from across the country, ranging in age from sixty to one hundred years old. They come from wide-ranging backgrounds: big cities to rural towns; native born and immigrant; wealthy to modest income; and retired from a variety of occupations, including teacher, nurse, homemaker, business executive, and security alarm installer. I did my best to balance factors such as gender, age, economic background, race, religion, and types of personal interests.

I sent each person the same ten questions to ponder before our interview. Then we talked by phone with an audio recorder rolling. We covered their childhoods, family life, paid and volunteer work, and current pursuits. We discussed what brings them joy and what role, if any, faith plays in their lives. We also delved into the barriers and setbacks they've faced. Were these joyful people just the lucky ones who had escaped hardship in life? They certainly were not. My interviewees bravely revealed wrenching past experiences of alcoholism, depression, divorce, abuse, getting fired, caring for a sick spouse, losing a child, and more. Despite all the challenges, they still chose joy.

After each interview I felt exhilarated and inspired by the stories people shared. A few common themes stood out. First, the majority of interviewees thought their lives were uninteresting and unimpressive. Yet I often found myself moved to tears hearing about the challenging life events from which they chose to create beauty, meaning, and goodness. As we spoke, I marveled at their perseverance, optimism, and love. The lives they thought of as ordinary were fascinating and impressive because of *how* these folks lived.

Another common trait: these people *intentionally* created the lives they wanted, particularly after hard times. Most were very articulate about how they had consciously chosen joy and purpose, then made a plan to achieve it.

A final point that stood out was how many people named faith or spirituality as playing an important role in their lives. For some, this meant following the call of a particular religious tradition. Many others described self-defined spiritual practices, such as time in nature and meditation or other mindfulness tools. Rarely did people name their religious affiliation or denomination. Instead, they focused on how their belief system was guiding them to live a better life.

I confess to falling in love with these people and their stories. Bits and pieces of their wisdom have woven themselves into my daily habits and thought processes. For example:

- Each morning, when I do a series of physical therapy stretches, I think of Dave, who told me, "I don't need any gym to work out in! I was in the navy. I know how to do floor exercises, and that's what I do every day." Me too, Dave!
- Stan's advice to choose to see what you *must* do each day as your daily purpose struck a deep chord for me. While managing my family of five, I've playfully called myself a "domestic goddess" when doing the daily work to keep my household functioning. Stan's words profoundly affirmed my choice to see necessary, repetitive chores as meaningful work.
- Stories of forgiveness, like that of Mary, who found peace after a decades-long rift with her brother, nudge me to consider relationships of my own that need attention and more love.

This journey started when I was a concerned and curious thirteen-year-old girl. Now I'm in my late fifties— old enough to really want to figure out how to age well. If you're picking up this book, you probably want to figure it out too. Thanks to the wisdom shared by those I interviewed for *Choose Joy* and years of research on positive aging, I've learned that aging well means being physically and mentally healthy, pursuing activities that give you purpose, and having loving relationships with friends and family. The people I interviewed are living examples of what the research tells us: tending to these three areas of your life will help you be happier, healthier, and live longer.

The interviewees cautioned, though, about what can happen if you don't make a plan for joy. It's common to have a honeymoon phase of retirement when sleeping in, drinking coffee, reading the paper, and working out feel like happy luxuries. But soon those luxuries shift into a feeling that something is missing, which can lead to tough stuff. Depression affects more than 6.5 million of the 35 million Americans aged sixty-five or older.[1] Research suggests that substance use is an emerging public health issue among the nation's older adults, with the number of older Americans with substance use disorder expected to rise from 2.8 million in 2002–2006 to 5.7 million by 2020.[2] And the divorce rate for adults fifty and older has roughly doubled since 1990, despite divorce rates decreasing for younger adults.[3] To avoid this dark side of retirement, we need to make a plan to live with joy now.

---

[1] "Depression in Older Persons," National Alliance on Mental Illness Minnesota, March 2017, https://namimn.org/wp-content/uploads/sites/188/2018/05/DepressionInOlderPersons_Ill nesses_Adult_2018.pdf.

[2] "A Day in the Life of Older Adults: Substance Use Facts," *CBHSQ Report*, Substance Abuse and Mental Health Services Administration, May 11, 2017, https://www.samhsa.gov/data/sites/default/files/report_2792/Shor tReport-2792.html.

[3] Renee Stepler, "Led by Baby Boomers, Divorce Rates Climb for America's 50+ Population," *Fact Tank*, Pew Research Center, March 9, 2017, https://www.pewresearch.org/fact-tank/2017/03/09/led-by-baby-boomers-divorce-rates-climb-for-americas-50-population.

The people in *Choose Joy* didn't just wake up on their eightieth birthdays and decide to get physically fit and do meaningful things. They made intentional choices in their fifties, sixties, and seventies to build habits, passions, and relationships that make aging well possible. My interviewees also did a powerful, counterculture thing: they ignored the outdated stereotypes of what retirement looks like, either idyllic, leisure-only images of golf, beaches, and cruise ships or grim pictures of frail older adults isolated and alone. Instead, they figured out what they love to do and did more of it. They chose joy.

These folks aren't doing huge things like climbing Mount Everest or founding nonprofits. They're simply making conscious choices to live with joy and meaning. And most of these choices require no money to pursue; they just take time and cultivation of a mindset.

The stories in *Choose Joy* focus on three keys to investing your time in retirement and help you answer critical questions about how to structure your time each week:

- Engage Your Mind: *What Are You Doing Monday Morning?*
- Move Your Body: *How Do You Want to Stay in Motion?*
- Connect with Others: *Who You Gonna Call?*

Like so many of us who have been caught in the busyness of raising families and pursuing careers, you might find it hard to remember what you used to love to do, but you can choose joy too. Here's how! Look to the stories in this book for fifty specific ideas of how ordinary people are living well in retirement. To help you translate these ideas into your own life, I offer a "Try This" idea after each story. These suggestions are tiny steps you might take to explore how you want to spend your time. If you want to dig even deeper, take advantage of the free resources that go along with this book. Just go to http://babs-@babsplunkett.com/choosejoy to get the free step-by-step guide to create your "Plan to Choose Joy."

I hope these ideas will inspire you to make your own choice to live joyfully. Not every story will be a match for every reader, but if you find even a few ideas that spark joy, you can be happier, be healthier, and live longer.

Let's get started!

ENGAGE YOUR MIND

What Are You Doing Monday Morning?

Do something that uses your gifts, not just fills your time.
—Joy, 80 years

I retired with not much money, but a whole lot of time, so that's what I give.
—John, 62 years

When we're working, most of us know exactly what we will be doing every Monday morning. That structure gives our days purpose and often defines a big part of our identity. In retirement, that built-in structure is gone and many of us experience a real loss, which can lead to dark times. But the loss of structure and a fixed identity is also an opportunity to explore new ways to engage your mind and structure your days with meaningful pursuits.

Some of the people I spoke with entered their post-career lives with a clear plan of how they wanted to spend their time. A year or two before retirement, they got involved with organizations that they cared about or started new hobbies. When their careers ended, they easily transitioned into bigger roles in organizations or spent more time on their hobbies.

Many others were not such long-range planners. Instead, they sampled classes, activities, and volunteer roles for a few years until they found a rhythm that felt right for them. Most didn't find just one big thing that filled their lives with purpose. Rather, they curated an engaging collection of interests that gave their lives meaning.

Research clearly supports the value of engaging our minds. "Having a purpose—engagement and working towards a goal as we age—is important for longevity, productivity, and lower rates of cognitive decline, stroke, and heart attack," according to Patricia Boyle of the Rush Alzheimer's Disease Center at Rush University Medical Center.[4] Even as few as one hundred hours of paid or volunteer work per year can have a positive effect on people's health. That's just two hours per week!

In this section, you will read about people volunteering, pursuing art or music, and learning new things. You'll also hear about people who took a completely different route and kept working in their retirement years. Each person found their own way to engage their mind in this new phase of life.

---

[4] Patricia Boyle et al., "Effect of Purpose in Life on the Relation between Alzheimer Disease Pathologic Changes on Cognitive Function in Advanced Age," *Archives of General Psychiatry*, 69 (2012).

DO SOMETHING FOR OTHERS

1

Volunteering Keeps Him Going
Grandpa Bob, 87 years

B ob grew up in New Orleans, where he got a rough start as a gang member. When the violence got worse, he joined the military to get away from the gang. As life unfolded further, Bob took a variety of jobs, including janitor, truck driver, and roofer. Of all the roles he's played in life, his favorite is that of Grandpa Bob in the Foster Grandparent Program, which pairs older adults with at-risk youth to boost kids' self-esteem and overall success. The program provides a small stipend to volunteers, so it offers a great way to give back and earn a little extra income, too.

Through Foster Grandparent, Grandpa Bob spends four days a week volunteering in the preschool of a nonprofit that helps single moms earn a college degree. The kids love his deep chuckle and sparkling eyes and always call him "Grandpa." He says, "The kids come to me and say, 'Grandpa Bob, come do a puzzle with me.' Or they want to do some kind of game, and if I have to get down on the floor to play, I'll do it. Now, it might not be easy to get back up"—he laughs—"but I'll do it! It's just fun being with them."

Grandpa Bob dedicates four hours to the program every day despite having prostate cancer, congestive heart failure, obstructed bowel, and asthma. He also nursed his wife for seven years. "People say, 'How can you keep doing this?' And I say, 'Get up in the morning and go!' I don't always feel good when I get up, but I get up and go anyway and always feel better when I get there. I like the kids, and if I didn't volunteer and keep going, I wouldn't be here now."

One morning, he helped a little girl in the program, D'Angela, solve a puzzle, gently suggesting how to match the colors and shapes. When she finally succeeded, D'Angela threw her little arms around his big frame and gave him a warm squeeze. Those happy exchanges happen every day he's with the kids.

Grandpa Bob's joyful story doesn't end there. After his wife passed away, a woman from his church offered to help him clear away his wife's things. "Well, we sort of bonded. Then we fell in love," says Grandpa Bob with a twinkle. "So, then we got married last year at age eighty-six! Some people say, 'Oh, that's too soon.' And I say, at my age, what am I waiting for?!"

TRY THIS

Does working with kids sound appealing to you? If so, do a quick search to see if there's a Foster Grandparent program near you. If there is no program nearby, check with your neighborhood school or library about tutoring, story time reading, or other requests for volunteers.

2

Award-Winning Smoke Detector Installers
Mary and Tom, 81 years

Mary and Tom searched hard for a volunteer role they could do together, that also allowed them the flexibility to travel regularly. They found their perfect match through the Red Cross and the Retired and Senior Volunteer Program (RSVP). The two non-profits collaborate on a program that identifies people in need of a smoke detector throughout Staten Island and sends volunteers to install one. Mary and Tom had no experience with installing smoke detectors, but they learned on the job so they could serve together.

Every month the program passes along the contact list to Mary and Tom. Mary then sets the installation appointment with each client at a time that works for Mary and Tom's busy schedules. The couple then travels together to the client's home to install the smoke detector and provide some social connection.

"Very often it's a single woman that we're helping, and I think it's much more comfortable to have a woman present when a man is coming into her home. I always let people know that two of us will be coming," explains Mary. Their clients vary, but most of them cannot climb a ladder due to physical limitations or do not feel comfortable doing so because they live alone. Mary adds, "We meet wonderful, interesting people, and they always like to chat."

Mary and Tom have dedicated more than five hundred hours over twelve years to installing smoke detectors for older adults and received a humanitarian award for their volunteer commitment. After fifty-nine years of marriage, volunteering together has given them a shared passion for helping those in need.

TRY THIS

If volunteering interests you, write down what skills you want to share and how you hope the experience will be fulfilling for you. Do you want to meet people? Work directly with clients? Connect virtually with people? It can take a few tries to find the right match, but if your list of criteria is clear, you'll be able to determine which opportunities are right for you. Nonprofits like the United Way offer one-stop shopping for volunteer opportunities.

3
Tikkun Olam, Heal the World
Barbara, 75 years

Barbara lives by the concept from her Jewish faith of *tikkun olam,* which means "heal the world." "The point is you've been given life," she says, "so you're supposed to do good for others in any small way you can."

As a single mom, she had no extra time or money to do good for others when her son was young. In fact, one day, when her son fell and ripped his pants, Barbara started crying because she didn't have enough money to replace them. Her little son got his piggy bank out and gave it to her, saying, "Here, Mommy, I don't want you to cry." In that moment Barbara thought to herself, "I've got to get another job, and someday I'm going to be able to give back to others."

Now that her son is grown, she is giving back. Barbara does her part for tikkun olam by doing *mitzvahs*—good deeds done with no expectation of anything in return. She found a nonprofit in New York City that lets you go online and choose short-term projects. "You get to pick whatever you like. I've worked in the library and done after school programs for children. I've served meals and sorted clothes for the homeless. For a long time, I did recordings for the blind. When the volunteer role isn't fulfilling anymore, I find something else. It's whatever I want to do in the timespan that I have."

One of her favorite mitzvahs took place at Christmas. She knew of a man who dressed up as Santa each year and gave toys to kids from a low-income area. Barbara liked to fill up a bag with cookies and other treats and put it by the door in his building with a card reading, "Thank you from the elves." She remembers, "People would say, 'Why don't you tell him it's you?' And I said, 'Because then it won't be a good deed! He'll keep thanking me and I'll feel embarrassed,'" Barbara says. "It's not something I can explain. I just want to do it. A mitzvah is something you do out of the goodness of your heart."

She adds, "You can really wrap yourself up in a cocoon of your own problems and get lost there. Doing for others takes you out of yourself and makes you happier."

TRY THIS

Choose one mitzvah, or good deed, to do today—and do it. Compliment the cashier at the grocery. Shovel or rake for your neighbor. Send a note to someone to let them know you're thinking of them. Then, notice how you feel for the rest of the day. Do you want to get more of that good feeling?

PURSUE A PASSION

4
Do What You Love
Molly, 70 years

Molly grew up in a big city, but as a little girl she always loved being around animals in the country because it made her feel grounded. Today, she connects to that feeling by raising a small menagerie of birds at home in Madison, Wisconsin. For years she has bred canaries, sometimes so successfully that ten cages filled her living spaces. Today she has just one cage and mates the pair each spring. Once the eggs hatch, Molly creates a cement-like mixture of chicken eggs, broccoli, and other nutritious foods for the parents to eat and feed their babies. It's a lot of work to feed, clean, and care for the birds, but Molly loves it. "I just enjoy the miracle of birth," she exclaims. "It's peaceful to listen to them learn to sing, from gargling to warbling."

Molly also raises chickens beside her city home. One year after retirement she had a chicken coop built. "I love having animals around, and I love the eggs," she says. "It's like finding a present every day! It makes me happy to have a little gift to give others." She confesses that caring for living things takes work, so it's not all bucolic; raccoons have eaten some of her hens, and the replacement hens have given harsh meaning to the term *pecking order*. These difficulties don't faze Molly, though. "It's fun to watch their personalities emerge. And they're companionable. Eventually they follow you around like a pet."

Another source of grounding for Molly is making pottery. Each fall she hits the pottery wheel for a few months to create Christmas gifts. She started a few years before retirement because she wanted to use the creative side of her brain as an antidote to a job that was very "heady" and stressful. "I haven't made a lot of progress," notes Molly with a laugh, "but I've always liked art that's useful. And there's no better feeling than when you're molding something in your hands, and it turns out wonderfully." Part of what drives Molly to keep at pottery is the knowledge that she may get arthritis someday, so she wants to do finger skills while she can.

On top of all these hobbies, Molly also dabbles at learning the harp. "Maybe it's the Irish in me," she jokes, "but I've always loved the harp." With self-deprecating humor, Molly claims she's not very accomplished, even after taking lessons on and off for twenty years. Her current goal is to learn enough repertoire to be able to perform at senior centers. In the meantime, Molly notes that research shows learning to read music is good brain training and discipline. "It feels good to keep my brain working in ways it usually doesn't," she says. "Playing an instrument is a good dynamic as I age. It's a gift I can give myself and others."

Pursuing hobbies that she loves grounds and delights Molly. "I realize there's always more to be learned and skills to be increased."

TRY THIS

Journal about what you loved to do or dreamed of doing as a child. If you can't remember, ask a family member or longtime friend. Grant yourself permission to try one of those activities. Don't worry about doing it well. Just do it for fun.

5
If You Look for the Good, You'll Find It
Jo, 68 years

Jo was diagnosed with depression when she was a young girl. In her teens and twenties, she sought out therapy to help her manage the depression and developed a lifelong practice to support her mental health. "I've been very cognizant of my depression for the rest of my life, trying to be alert to symptoms of when I might be going down the dark hole and taking steps to avert that," Jo explains.

One critical time the dark hole opened was when Jo was a young mother. The depression was so severe that Jo realized she could harm her babies. "I became aware of that inner voice that starts and says, 'I'm not good enough,' or 'I'm not adequate and won't measure up to my siblings,'" she says. "During that time, and still today, when I start hearing that internal message, I have to stop—shut off the garbage. When I'm thinking of the ugly things in me, then I know I'm *really* thinking too much about myself. It's time to think outside about others."

Fortunately, during that time Jo got additional therapy help, which she credits with saving her and her children. "I'm really grateful for the treatment 'cuz, like I said, I could've really done damage to my kids. I'm sure they have some scars, but thankfully I got help early and started working with the tools I was given."

Now sixty-eight years old, Jo has dedicated her life to staying emotionally healthy by focusing on the positive and living intentionally.

In each of her life stages, Jo's faith led her to believe we all have different vocations, depending on our place and time. Following that call helped her maintain her emotional health. "I had a vocation to be a wife and mother. I also had this side thing happening with being the music director at church. And another side thing with my paid work. But my *vocation* was to be a wife and mother," explains Jo. "For me, a vocation is a serious calling, and it's a commitment."

To discover her next vocation in retirement, Jo did a training program at her church named "Called & Gifted," a three-part workshop for discerning spiritual gifts. "The program crystallized a few things for me. It helped me understand that I have many talents that I've taken for granted. Now I see that there's a purpose for me to use those gifts for others. It's not just for my own personal satisfaction." Jo defined her gifts as teaching, music, and administration, all skills she had used throughout her paid and volunteer work. But now she felt a calling to share those gifts in new ways with others.

To engage her gift for administration, she serves on a board and as a Lions Club member. She uses her musical gifts as a part-time music director for her church choir. And the precious time she dedicates every week to her grandkids is infused with opportunities to teach as she reads with the kids or brings them to concerts and plays.

"In retirement, I get to look for the good and incorporate all my gifts—gifts that were always there—but now I realize it's my higher purpose to use them." Jo adds, "I have chosen to be a Pollyanna. Yes, the bad stuff is there. But if you look for the good, you'll find it."

TRY THIS

Put on your rose-colored glasses and look for the good in your life for thirty minutes. Write down all the good things you can see in your life right now. List the simple gifts you have to give others. Which of those gifts is nudging you to give it some attention?

6

Make a Plan, Live It, Revise As Needed
Simin, 69 years

B eneath Simin's calm, elegant exterior is a power-house of purpose. As a petite female immigrant from Iran, Simin defied all the stereotypes of a technology leader during her thirty-year career at a major university. She put in ten-hour days managing more than a hundred people, starting in the era of mainframe computers and ending with laptops and tablets. She achieved this while raising three children, including a daughter with special needs. Simin was always busy and loved it.

As retirement approached, Simin made a conscious choice to get involved with some organizations before she left her fast-paced job. "I *knew* I'd go crazy if I didn't have something set up," Simin says. "Because I started working with the organizations before I left the university, I was able to continue on with something. There was never a time of doing nothing."

One of Simin's favorite volunteer roles is working with Sister Cities International for a town in France. As a board member she helps plan student exchanges and inter-cultural events. "I just love the work I do with Sister City projects," she exclaims. "I've made fabulous relationships and feel like my brain has expanded in knowledge." She also gets to combine her love of music and French by planning fundraising events to support a music competition in France. "This volunteer work energizes me and fills my days with a feeling of accomplishment."

Working with Sister Cities also helps Simin connect to retirement dreams that have not gone according to plan. "I always wanted to go to France with my husband and stay for a couple of months to use my French," Simin says. "I also wanted time to play piano and practice my harp." Early in retirement, however, her mother's health took a turn that demanded daily care from Simin. Simin now dedicates four hours every day to helping her homebound mother with food and household management. She also helps to feed, bathe, and dress her special-needs daughter every day. "We all have distractions in our plans that are out of our control. I had to ask myself, 'Can I manage to achieve what I want while dealing with the distractions?' I decided I can, with a supportive family and a willingness to work hard."

Simin credits three choices for helping her accomplish what she wants to achieve. First, she reframed the time spent caring for her mother and daughter as a main source of purpose and satisfaction. She is choosing to make her caregiving work part of her life purpose right now. Second, Simin takes time for her music, squeezing piano practice into any spare moment, even if it's just fifteen minutes while dinner is simmering. Finally, she seeks out volunteer roles that refuel her energy. "I feel like every organization I've joined has added more to me than I have contributed to them. The work energizes me. There's such a sense of satisfaction in what I do. I'd be totally lost in retirement without this work."

Simin's retirement dreams haven't unfolded exactly as planned, but by reframing her vision and working hard, she's still always busy and loving it.

TRY THIS

A first step in creating a plan for retirement is deciding if you want to continue using the skills from your career, explore a new skill set, or both. List the skills you excel at and love best from your work. Can you get paid for those skills? Do you want to give them freely? What new skills pique your curiosity? Could you start learning one today?

GET CREATIVE

7
Music in the Key of Life
Bob, 84 years

Music has been the resonating chord throughout Bob's life. He started playing the trombone in sixth grade and continued all through college. He even played in a dance band early in his marriage, until the demands of his career and his family took precedence. During those busy years, Bob kept his chops up by playing in a community band, where the time commitment was more modest.

After the kids were grown and launched, Bob increased his commitment to music, playing for joy and friendship. His bandmates were a balm during the fifteen years of his wife's battle with Alzheimer's, from her diagnosis at just fifty-nine years old until her death. "That was a really tough time," Bob recalls. "I retired in 1998 to take care of her. Did that for several years until it was too hard. Then she lived a few years more. That's just not the way it's supposed to happen. But it did. And you just have to deal with it." Music helped Bob carry on.

Today, music is more present than ever in Bob's life. He still plays in the community band, and for ten years he has also played weekly in a brass quintet with musicians ranging in age from thirty-five to eighty-four years. They perform regularly at senior centers and get bar gigs three or four times a year. "I think I'm playing better with age. I get more musical versus just playing the right notes."

Laughing, he adds, "But you do need good teeth, and my teeth are okay!"

Bob complements his own music with a passion for opera. He attends performances in Denver, his hometown, and travels to enjoy other productions. The day before we spoke, Bob had attended an opera in a small town west of Denver that has hosted an opera festival since the 1800s. "It was a Verdi blockbuster that was magnificent! The theater is small, five hundred seats, so I was right smack-dab up against the performers. It was such a high I couldn't sleep that night," he exclaims. Bob often shares his love of opera with his lady friend, Nancy. One time, the couple traveled to San Francisco to see Wagner's *Ring Cycle*, a fifteen-hour epic production that runs for a week. "It was wonderful! And it's fun to share my love of opera with Nancy." Bob laughs again and notes, "I don't drink much, I don't swear, and I don't chase women, but I do love opera!"

Bob has also passed along his love of opera by teaching a course for the Osher Lifelong Learning Institute (OLLI) in his area. OLLI offers noncredit courses in art, science, sports, history, and current events in 122 programs nationwide. Every winter for the past twenty years Bob has offered a class exploring eight operas in eight weeks. "It keeps my mind going and prepares me for my next opera trip."

TRY THIS

It's never too late to learn an instrument. It's good for the brain and great for the spirit. You can find lessons in community education, at a local music school, or online. If music appreciation is more your thing, check out OLLI or your nearest college for opportunities to listen and learn. Write down three options that appeal to you and try them out.

8

Tools for Living
Sharon, 76 years

Sharon was sixty-eight when her husband passed away after fifty years of marriage. It was his birthday. Then, two years later to the day, her forty-eight-year-old daughter died by suicide. Time stopped. "It was a foggy emotional time. That level of loss is a strange thing that's hard to explain," Sharon says. She coped as she could. It was a grey and dreary January in Michigan as the one-year anniversary of her daughter's death approached. Sharon felt a strong gut instinct to retreat to someplace warm for the anniversary. She googled "spiritual retreats," found an appealing match, and booked her flights.

"The retreat center had incredible practitioners that helped me with my healing," Sharon says. Journaling, meditation, and yoga were already part of Sharon's life at home, so it felt natural to deepen those practices on the retreat. She worked through many guided healing activities, releasing the pain and sadness of losing her daughter and husband and moving toward lightness. The week culminated in a candle-lighting ritual to honor her daughter, husband, and parents.

This restorative time left her feeling more peaceful and confident than she had in a very long time. Sharon says, "The gift from the difficult years is realizing I'd spent my whole life living with my parents or husband, always needing to check in with them on decisions. Earlier in my life I don't think I would've trusted my intuition to search retreats, book airline tickets, and go. I now realize *I trust me*! It turns out I'm brilliant at decision making."

After the retreat, Sharon was ready to reconstruct that part of herself that she hadn't taken care of while raising a family and managing a career. Through journaling, she took herself back in time to ask curious questions about who she was before she was a wife and mother. What did I like to do as a child? What did I want to do as a young woman? What were the good parts of my childhood? In exploring her past, she remembered that she used to love to draw, so she has started taking art classes and drawing every day. "I'm absolutely joyful when I'm drawing, pursuing something I love." Sharon counts drawing as one of her "tools for living," things that put her in touch with her greatest level of contentment.

Another of her tools for living is playing the piano, which she quit when she left high school. "I decided to take piano lessons again," she says with a sparkle. "But heaven help the lady who was trying to teach me! I think I learned better as a child." Her other tools are meditation, yoga, time with her family, and a passion for genealogy.

"On a typical day I wake up, meditate, draw, and then go where the day leads me," says Sharon. "I had to learn this skill after a lifetime of daily and weekly goals. I do have a bigger goals list that I check on when it works. But most days I follow the flow of the day." Sharon's tools for living helped her realize that she needed to "stop looking for happiness as a goal. It's a side effect of being peaceful and grounded."

TRY THIS

Doodle for fifteen minutes about your tools for living. What brings you great contentment? Movement? Music? Cooking? Camping? Your drawings don't need to be fine art. Just play with the pen or pencil to rediscover what you used to love doing.

9
World Music Radio DJ
Marta, 78 years

Marta's love of world music accidentally landed her a spot as a volunteer radio DJ. Decades ago, when her husband worked at Michigan State University, Marta enjoyed listening to the college radio station, which happened to be one of the strongest radio programs in the country at the time. She called in and asked them to consider playing music from the countries represented by the many international students at the university. When the station manager said they didn't know anything about that music, she replied, "If you find someone, I'd be happy to help them out." That was all the manager needed to hear to persuade Marta to be that person. She jumped in and started producing a thirty-minute show, learning the radio ropes as she went along.

A few years later, when her husband took a job at the University of Chicago, Marta volunteered at that college radio station, which broadcasts throughout the South Side's culturally diverse neighborhoods. "It's nice to be in contact with students and community people. This station is a place where people can share the music they love." Marta continues to share her love of international music and culture through her weekly *Music around the World* radio show.

"I'm happy people like the sound of the world music. But what I'm really interested in is the culture that the music is a part of. My radio show is like Intro to Anthropology," jokes Marta. "I throw in information about how the music fits in with the culture. (Some say too much info!) I'm not talking about what the lyrics mean, but about the role of music in each culture." Often, Marta tries to connect her musical selections with world events. If a particular immigrant group or political conflict is in the news, she'll play music from that culture.

Marta believes music can connect and inform us. "People might not go to a lecture on Islam. But, if I play Indonesian music and mention that Indonesia has the largest Islamic population in the world, followed by India, Pakistan, and Bangladesh, they might be surprised that a Middle Eastern country isn't on that list. Maybe they'll remember that little fact in the future," she says.

For more than fifty years, Marta has shared her love of world music on the airwaves. Recently it's gotten a bit harder for her as she recovers from cancer surgery, but she keeps at it because she loves exposing people to new music. A few years ago, a man called in and told Marta, "I didn't want to listen to your show, but my wife left the radio on while I was doing my woodworking. My hands were covered in goo, so I couldn't change the channel. But I found out I liked it!" That listener connection keeps her on the air.

TRY THIS

What subject would you love to share with others? There are six hundred college radio stations nationwide if you want to broadcast widely. If you'd rather start smaller, consider teaching a community ed course. Or simply gather some friends in person or virtually for an information swap where each person presents for five to ten minutes about their favorite topic.

UNRETIRE

10

Law School at Age 56
Gerry, 79 years

Gerry jokes that he wants his tombstone to say, "He was flexible." His twisting career path started in data processing, moved to owning a resort, and culminated with becoming an attorney in his late fifties.

Right out of college, Gerry went to work for the Pillsbury Company in Minneapolis at a time when they had just ordered their first mainframe computer. He spent the next decade working in the data processing field (later called information technology or IT) during its boom years. As the technology culture shifted and layoffs began, Gerry and his wife, Bev, decided to leave big-city life and raise their four girls at a slower pace. Having met as childhood sweethearts in a rural area, they knew the joys of small-town life.

To make the move work, Gerry and Bev got the idea to open a resort. "We'd never stayed in a resort," Bev confesses. "But Gerry had a business degree and I had a home ec degree, so we thought we could do it." They found the ideal resort right in their own hometown of Crosslake, Minnesota, population 2,141. The resort was called The Hollywood Inn because the first owners spent their winters in California working for Hollywood celebrities. Gerry and Bev didn't feel Hollywood matched their personalities, so they changed the name slightly to the Holly Woods Resort. They put everything they had into it, including all their savings, and got started.

"The first year Bev taught school in the off-season to add income," explains Gerry. "I stayed home and cooked from my mother's cookbook. The girls didn't love my cooking." He laughed at that. After this first year, an opportunity arose for Gerry to do IT consulting. He got an October-through-April contract that allowed him to work at the resort in the summer. For the next twelve years, Gerry and Bev enjoyed running the resort with their girls. From fishing opener in May to October 1, they had fun working together to prep and clean the ten little cabins, run the resort store that sold candy, bait, and fishing licenses, and build friendships with their guests.

When the girls went off to college, it was hard to find good workers, and the fun began to wear thin. Gerry and Bev decided to redevelop the resort into condos, a choice that proved fateful. The effort led to a protracted lawsuit. The contentious fight made Gerry remember when he was eight years old and his dad said, "You argue like a Philadelphia lawyer." He'd always thought he'd like to do that. That lawsuit shaped the third twist in Gerry's flexible career.

At age fifty-six, Gerry went to law school, finishing by age fifty-eight. He then interned with the firm that had handled his lawsuit. When he passed the bar exam, Gerry opened a branch in his hometown and has practiced real estate law ever since. He plans to retire soon at age eighty.

"I've found satisfaction in the variety of my career path," says Gerry. "When I see an opportunity, I take it." He adds, "There isn't just one way to live a satisfactory life. There are many, many ways to do it."

TRY THIS

"Second chapter" careers are a great way to stay engaged. What job have you always wished you could try? There's still time to get training or a degree if needed. Your next birthday will come whether you pursue your dream job or not. Celebrate by taking the first step in your next career.

11

The Fun of the Sale
Bob and Mary, 88 years and 86 years

Throughout their sixty-three years of marriage, Bob and Mary have always loved the thrill of competition. Whether it's closing a big sale or simply betting a dollar on their weekly tennis game (yes, they still play), they see competition and sales as a fun, lifelong game.

Bob's career in media sales launched at the same time as television advertising. He sold TV ads during the network boom and then moved into the next new thing: cable. He even helped invent the infomercial for a small start-up sports channel called ESPN.

When Bob finally retired, he and Mary moved from Chicago to a retirement community in Savannah, Georgia, where he diverted his love of competition into playing golf six days per week and tennis four days per week. "And then Mary said to me, 'Is that all you're gonna do?!'" Bob recalls with an amused chuckle. Taking his wife's advice, he looked around and discovered that their community TV station needed an ad rep. The scale was certainly different from ESPN, but the thrill of the sales challenge was still the same. Bob went back to work, and he's been there for fourteen years.

"I absolutely love it!" Bob exclaims. "I love to win, and I like to make sales." He also realizes that working gives him a sense of purpose. "Some of the guys have told me they're jealous that I can still work." Bob has now worked in sales for sixty-three years and plans to keep selling as long as he can.

"He'd like to be the world's oldest salesman, so I don't think he'll retire," Mary interjects with a smile. This works for both of them because Mary hasn't retired either.

Although Mary has never seen herself as a business-woman, she started her jewelry business in the early 1960s, when their kids were young. A friend had planned a jewelry party to sell pieces she'd brought back from Greece and encouraged Mary to make some necklaces to sell at the party, too. Mary's jewelry sold out, but the Greek pieces remained. Mary realized she was on to something.

By the mid-1970s, Mary was hosting her own jewelry sales parties. Sales were so strong that she started selling to high-end boutiques such as Neiman Marcus. "I never thought of this as work," Mary says. "It's more of a hobby, and I love it. *Love it!* I sit down at eight, next thing I know it's noon, then the next thing I know it's five. I never, ever tire of this." For fifty years Mary has made and sold her jewelry. "My friends think it's unbelievable that I'm still working. But it's wonderful."

Bob and Mary agree that continuing to work has been a great way to stay engaged and connected in the community. Bob adds, "There are ten thousand people in our community. Through Mary's jewelry sales and me being so visible through the ad sales, people know us. So that's kinda fun. We're lucky!"

TRY THIS

Write down which part of your career you loved the most. What skill area left you feeling energized? Explore how you could keep sharing that skill. Maybe your current or previous employer needs part-time support. If you want to start fresh, a small business or nonprofit might value your contribution.

12

"Failed" Retirement
Eileen, 87 years

I have failed retirement," laughs Eileen. She has tried to retire so many times that her kids joke they'll never go to another retirement party for her again.

She first retired at age seventy from a career in nursing and nursing education. Two weeks after retiring, her parish priest asked her to help start a parish nursing program to care for the physical and spiritual needs of the people in their church community. For the next eight years Eileen served forty-five clients in a part-time, paid role, though she volunteered countless additional hours to meet demand.

At age seventy-eight, Eileen retired from that job, only to get hired to run a nursing program at an assisted-living center. She chuckles remembering that she was the same age as many of her clients. During her two years in this job, Eileen also taught classes on health-care topics and got more deeply involved with hospice.

Some of Eileen's most powerful work was born out of the pain and healing from a tragic event she endured. Her son, Will, suffers from schizophrenia and could become dangerously violent during psychotic episodes. One summer day the unthinkable happened. In the darkness of his schizophrenia, Will killed his father. Will pled guilty and was sentenced to twenty-five years in prison. Eileen calls the years following the tragedy "a long siege." She coped with a collision of emotions and navigated legal processes while helping her other children endure the ordeal. Eileen reflects tearfully on the struggle she wrestled with then and continues to live with every day. "As a person of faith, I had to ask myself, how many times do I have to forgive? The Bible says we should 'forgive each other seventy times seven.' Although the pain lives on, I decided to forgive."

Eileen's forgiveness led her to establish a hospice program for the inmates at Will's prison that is still going strong today. To find some purpose in the tragedy, she also became a lead volunteer for the state chapter of the National Alliance on Mental Illness (NAMI), a national organization dedicated to improving the lives of people affected by mental illness. She ultimately became president of the board for NAMI. In this role, Eileen advocated to get a bill passed that allows families to intervene in mental health emergencies to put their loved one "on hold" for their safety. She hopes this will spare others from her pain.

Now eighty-seven years old, Eileen still has not retired. She keeps her nursing license up to date so she can continue teaching classes and making house calls in her neighborhood, noting, "I feel I can't make medical referrals unless I have that license to back me up." During this "failed" retirement Eileen has found great meaning and contributed to countless lives. Her kids will not have to worry about another retirement party any time soon.

TRY THIS

Are you part of the 23 percent of people who plan to keep working? Assess your budget, passion, and energy to determine if working full-time or part-time is right for you. Then research what skills, certifications, or ongoing training is necessary to continue working in your field.

TRY SOMETHING NEW

13

No Limits when You Set Them Yourself
Robin C., 82 years

In his early twenties, Robin sat on the stoop of his inner-city home in Flint, Michigan, waiting for people to notice how tough and cool he was. No one noticed. He realized nobody was going to come by and say, "Join us and be happy," so he made up his mind to find his own good in the world. Just a few years later, good came in an unexpected form: he got drafted.

"The army changed my life," Robin says, "because without the army, I probably would've stayed in the ghetto—our neighborhood. I probably wouldn't have gone anywhere or been exposed to so many new things." In basic training, Robin encountered people who'd been to Europe and could speak phrases in German. "I loved watching movies where people spoke German, so the first thing I did when I got out of the army was take a German class back home. We had a great time learning the language and hosting parties with the French club to sample the foods. I studied some French too."

The army in the late 1950s wasn't the easiest place for a Black man. Robin was stationed in Texas—not Europe or Hawaii as he'd hoped. "It was like the Deep South," he recalls. "I couldn't leave the post without people yelling at me and calling me names." Luckily, he discovered a roller rink on the post. He already loved roller skating, so he skated every day. There he met his friend Buddy, who was a show skater. Buddy taught Robin to do the Axel, a major jump. But even that bond was tested outside the rink. One time, Buddy invited Robin to a party off the base and even offered to double date. Buddy was white and didn't realize that it just wasn't an option for Robin.

When he finished his tour of duty, Robin returned home and kept skating. Roller skating led to figure skating, which led to downhill skiing. He invited his brothers and brothers-in-law to join him, but they all said, "Oh no, that's a white person's sport." Often, Robin was the only Black person in the rink or on the hill. Unfazed, he says, "It wasn't that difficult to be the only Black person in a traditionally white sport. If I wanted to be part of the group, I just tried to fit in, and people accepted me."

For years, Robin chose a new sport or subject each year to master. When computers were new, he got used parts and built one to learn how they work. (Being a professional electrician helped with that one.) Another year he grew curious about how male gymnasts do the scissors on a pommel horse (a difficult movement of swinging the legs over and around the horse). To figure it out, Robin built a pommel horse and taught himself that skill. Later, he decided to learn tae kwon do, eventually earning his red belt and then teaching his children the forms.

Today, Robin's passion is tai chi. He and his wife, Kathleen, take classes twice a week and practice every day at home. They've memorized five or six different forms and are advancing quickly, giving them the joy of sharing a passion. Robin described watching a video of a tai chi master who could use his energy to push a huge man off his feet. "He's just this little ol' guy from China, doing a push-pull movement, trying to move a big guy. The big guy just goes flying backward, while the master stayed rooted," Robin exclaims. "That's my passion now. I think I'd like to be a tai chi master."

All his life, Robin faced barriers due to race, but he chose to live by this motto: "There are no boundaries or limits when you set them yourself." He sets no limits for himself, so it will not be surprising if obstacles fly out of his path as he stays rooted in the knowledge that he's created his own good.

TRY THIS

What mental or physical limits have you unconsciously set for yourself? Are you ready to let those limits go? What have you always dreamed of doing but told yourself is impossible? Do it now. Book a class. Book a flight. Watch a YouTube video to learn a new skill. Take whatever action will get you started on that dream.

14

Do, Explore, Volunteer
Larry, 62 years

When Larry's pension kicked in at age sixty, he jumped at the chance to retire early. While he looked forward to not working, he realized he would miss three things from his job: structure, purpose, and community. So, he spent time thinking about how to recreate those three important components and settled on creating an activities binder.

Larry's activities binder is a simple tool with three tabs: Do, Explore, and Volunteer. The "Do" section is organized by seasons, with ideas and information about activities Larry loves doing or has always wanted to try, such as cross-country ski rentals, local theater listings, and spring baseball schedules. In the "Explore" tab, Larry gathers options ranging from new restaurant reviews to new biking trails to discover. The "Volunteer" tab contains Larry's notes on interesting opportunities; he consults it when he's ready for a change from his current commitments.

To develop fresh ideas for his activities binder, Larry used the "Get-a-Life Tree" exercise from Ernie Zelinski's book *How to Retire Happy, Wild, and Free*. In the exercise, Larry explored three questions: what does he like to do now, what did he like to do in the past, and what new ideas spark his interest? He wrote these three questions down to create the "trunk" of his tree. Then he wrote down answers as branches from that trunk, challenging himself to imagine at least fifty ideas without judgment. Larry focused on genuine interests and challenging activities that develop new skills. He regularly updates his Get-a-Life Tree to keep his activities binder full of appealing options.

By combining choices from his Do, Explore, and Volunteer categories, Larry leads an engaging life. He enjoys weekly and monthly volunteer roles, weekly bowling leagues, a monthly poker group, and standing biking times with friends. He also creates seasonal adventures, like the ten-day trip he orchestrates every spring with a group of friends to follow their favorite baseball team through minor league games in Rochester, Toronto, and Cleveland. Using his activities binder as a guiding tool, Larry has found structure, purpose, and community in his retirement.

TRY THIS

Create your own activities binder. Borrow the categories of Do, Explore, and Volunteer, or choose ones that reflect your own priorities, such as Body, Mind, and Spirit or Family, Fun, and Faith. Collect ideas for what brings you joy and meaning—and try them.

15

Aging Well Is a Decision You Make
Stan R., 84 years

Y ou know, I could sum up all your questions about how to age well with one statement: just decide to do it," Stan tells me halfway through our conversation.

"It's not easy to do, of course. But in my opinion, aging well is a decision you make." To keep himself motivated during the hard times, Stan applies his decades as a professor at the University of Kansas to his own life and does some research. He has read and absorbed countless books on hope, happiness, and how to build effective habits.

One book inspired Stan to define what makes him happy *today* and do it. He succinctly named the top three things that are currently making him happy: 1. Taking care of his wife, who has physical issues that limit her mobility. 2. Taking care of himself. 3. Accomplishing what needs to be done today. On the particular day that we spoke, Stan was choosing to accomplish the following: say his daily prayers, enjoy coffee and the paper, go to the office for a short task, meet up with a coffee group, take his wife to tai chi and share lunch, go to weight class, handle a financial chore, and then go to dinner with friends. While this may sound like a simple to-do list, Stan emphasizes that the point is to *choose* to see the value in whatever needs to be done. Framing his life from this angle brings him joy.

Taking care of his wife and himself make the list every day. After that, Stan follows the flow of whatever needs doing and takes satisfaction in getting it done.

Another book Stan mentioned is about making hope happen. "You can *hope* that you lose weight while you're eating poorly. Or, you can take some actions to fulfill your hope." Stan hopes to live to one hundred, so he's taking a lot of action to help him achieve that. In a typical week, Stan does two yoga classes, two weight classes, and two tai chi classes with his wife, spends four to five hours at the university mentoring young professors, joins his coffee group, goes to church, and has regular social time with friends.

Stan also gains wisdom from his friends. A favorite friend from his weight class, Neil, was a particular inspiration. Not only did Neil continue showing up at class during his chemotherapy, but he also printed business cards that read, "No Complaining on the Yacht." Stan tells me, "Neil believed you shouldn't strive to live the life you *love* because there are no guarantees your body will cooperate with being able to fish, golf, or travel. Instead, you should love the life you're living." Stan has made up his mind to love the life he lives, and he certainly never complains on the yacht.

TRY THIS

Choose three things that will make you happy today. Grant yourself permission to let the activities be anything from tackling a chore to contacting a friend, trying a daring new exploration, or taking a long nap. Go ahead and jot it down. Now do it!

MOVE YOUR BODY

How Do You Want to Stay in Motion?

Keep moving or you'll sludge up. —Bob, 84 years

To live well in retirement, we need to move our bodies. The people I interviewed made a commitment to stay in motion, even when they didn't feel like it, even when their bodies began to decline. They didn't keep moving because they're some special group of superheroes. They are just ordinary people who decided to make fitness a priority by building it into their daily and weekly schedules.

Most people chose familiar activities like walking, swimming, golf, yoga, or going to the gym. Others told me they had no interest in going to the gym or joining a fitness class; instead, they found ways to keep moving that matched their interests and values. Many made modifications as their bodies changed. They switched from high-intensity sports to gentler options, or they adapted their movement over time to accommodate an injury or new limitation. Still, they kept going.

There's good news for people pursuing any type of physical activity. A study published in the medical journal *Lancet* found that people who spent just 150 minutes each week (or about 20 to 30 minutes per day) were far less likely to suffer heart attacks, stroke, or cardiovascular disease and had a reduced risk of premature death.[5] The study suggested that simply walking and doing household chores for those 150 minutes has the same health impact as going to the gym.

In this section you will meet people who chop wood, haul brush, and tend their yards. You'll hear from others who "get their steps in" while volunteering with animals or homeless people. Still others stay active through local and international travel. Whether it's at the gym, in the yard, or far from home, these people find joy by staying in motion.

---

[5] Scott A. Lear et al., "The Effect of Physical Activity on Mortality and Cardiovascular Disease in 130,000 People from 17 High-Income, Middle-Income, and Low-Income Countries: The PURE Study," *Lancet* 390, no. 10113 (December 16, 2017): 2643–2654.

MOVE FOR
THE JOY OF IT

16

Act III Adventures
Robin D., 65 years

As retirement approached, Robin D. joined an athletic gang of friends in creating a travel group dubbed Act III Adventures. Their tongue-in-cheek tagline is "Cramming for the eulogy," fitting for a group that's packing in as much hiking, biking, camping, and fun as they can, while they can.

Every spring for the past five years, Act III Adventures has taken a biking trip somewhere in the United States. On one trip, members biked Moab and Four Arch Canyon in Utah. Every day they put in as many miles as they could, and every evening they relaxed and prepared meals together.

Alaska is the group's next destination. A few members have visiting every US national park on their bucket lists, so the plan to explore three of the state's eight national parks is a bonus. On a previous trip to Alaska, the friends encountered a grizzly bear (at a safe distance, but still thrilling). After the trip, Robin photoshopped the bear into the group's favorite selfie and used it as the cover for a photobook created for each couple.

Act III Adventures came together organically, with five main couples getting the travel idea rolling and a few folks floating in and out for different trips. Two of the couples are former neighbors. The others are friends of friends. Each couple takes a turn planning the logistics of a trip, and other members pitch in their special talents. For example, one creative person thought the group needed a logo, so she whipped one up. Then she produced T-shirts and a magnetic sign that they slap on the side of their rental vehicles.

"Act III Adventures is the kind of thing that keeps life interesting," says Robin. "It combines adventure, travel, and friends. What a nice trio!"

TRY THIS

What do you enjoy doing when you travel? Maybe it's high-energy exploration, or maybe it's more mellow activities like antiquing, bourbon tasting, or attending baseball openers. Think of one or more people who share that interest. Share this story and invite them to try a one-day group adventure. See where it leads you!

17

Dancing into a Second Career
Richard, 82 years

A cruise ship excursion changed Richard's life. After caring for his wife with early-onset Alzheimer's for ten years, Richard was so exhausted that his doctor ordered him to get full-time care for his wife and then take a cruise to restore his health.

On the trip, Richard rekindled his love of ballroom dance and discovered his calling as a dance host, a gentleman hired to dance with women traveling without a dance partner. Richard knew immediately that this was his future. He went home and took private lessons to bring up his skills while caring for his wife until the end.

Today, Richard is eighty-two years old and has worked as a dance host for fifteen years, though most hosts are forty to sixty-two years old. A typical evening for Richard begins with an hour of predinner dancing. Then he and the other hosts join guests for dinner to chat and encourage them to come dance. Dancing after dinner continues until midnight or 1:00 a.m. The nights are physically demanding but personally rewarding.

On one cruise, Richard noticed a woman in a wheelchair who clearly loved the music. With her permission, he and another dance host gently picked her up and moved her to the music. "She was absolutely elated!" Richard recalls.

Back home in Massachusetts, Richard performs in an accordion/voice duo at long-term care centers. During breaks, he plays recorded music and dances with the residents to share his joy. He also hones his own dancing skills, working to master the Argentine tango and competing in dance contests.

During the decade of caregiving for his wife, Richard couldn't imagine how he'd carry on. Joyful movement helped him dance his way into a new phase of life and a second career traveling the world.

TRY THIS

Now is the perfect time to "dance like nobody's watching." From the privacy of your home, you can try online classes for tap, hip-hop, and ballroom, and even how to dance like a Rockette. Go ahead and bust a move!

18

Exercise Body and Spirit
Peter, 92 years

Peter believes exercise is essential for your body and your spirit. By 5:30 each morning he's at the Y to start his day with a thirty-minute swim. He and other regulars chat and keep tabs on each other's swimming and daily lives.

Peter swam with his wife, Janet, until she became ill in her eighties. During the long months of caring for her, swimming gave Peter solace. "Swimming is literally prayer time for me," he says. "You know, swimming is *dull*—my body is swimming, but my mind isn't. So, my mind is free to pray while I swim."

After pool time and a breakfast banana, Peter continues his prayer time by walking to daily mass. After mass, he often walks a five-mile loop of the city. He started the loop as a challenge to himself, and now it's part of a daily discipline that combines fitness, social time, and meditation. Sometimes as he walks the city, he runs into old friends and strikes up a conversation. Other times he reflects in silence, saying a set of prayers as he moves.

After all this, Peter doesn't stop moving. Twice a week he also plays golf with a group of fifteen men; he's by far the oldest of them. "The younger men often say, 'Oh, I want to be as active as you are at ninety,'" Peter says. "But the thing they don't seem to understand is that they have to start *now*. I've been swimming my whole life and never stopped." He kept swimming even after back surgery in his sixties. "You can't just get old and decide to do something," Peter adds. "If you want to be active in your nineties, get moving now!"

TRY THIS

Many practices combine movement with meditation or prayer. Consider taking up tai chi, qigong, yoga, or martial arts, or search YouTube for videos on meditation exercises. Choose one or two to sample today.

GET YOUR STEPS IN WHILE GIVING

19

A Week in Action
Dorothy and Gordon, 90 years and 93 years

Dorothy and Gordon didn't start volunteering until after they retired. Today their weekly schedule is like a fitness routine at the gym. On Mondays and Fridays, the couple is on the move volunteering at an area hospital. Dorothy is a runner, shuttling supplies from one department to another. Gordon ran a cart of supplies around too, until his knees started complaining. Now he's contributing his time as a receptionist in the Nuclear Medicine Department.

Instead of pumping weights, Dorothy and Gordon hoist boxes of books. For the past decade they have dedicated Tuesdays and Wednesdays to helping operate Book 'Em, a seasonal book sale that raises funds for crime prevention in their city. An average shift is three hours of collecting, hauling, and sorting books, but as the sale approaches, they increase their time to help alphabetize the books and organize them into categories. During the sale, the couple is all-in, contributing five hours every day for the entire two-week sale. In a typical year, all that heavy lifting brings in $185,000 to fight crime.

There's no day of rest for these two. On Thursdays, Dorothy and Gordon serve as shoppers for a nonprofit that helps formerly-homeless people furnish their homes with everything they need for a fresh start. They walk a mile of warehouse aisles, helping clients choose everything from furniture to lamps to bedding and housewares. "I remember one homeless vet moving into the first home he'd had in *years*," Gordon says. "He couldn't believe how much he was getting for his new home. It just makes you grateful."

Dorothy and Gordon tried many volunteer options before finding matches for their values and passions. "I firmly believe in the power of staying active and positive," says Dorothy. "Find something you really enjoy, and do it! You might have to search for it, but just try something. I stay active enough today that I don't really need a fitness center anymore."

TRY THIS

Choose a cause that you care about, and call to learn about volunteer roles in it. Find one where you can stay active while volunteering, and give it a shot. See how it feels to move your body while giving. Imagine the satisfaction of getting your daily dose of exercise while helping others.

20

Buckthorn Removal Project
Jim N., 72 years

Jim used to bike to work along a creek and lake choked with buckthorn, a robust invasive species. When he retired two years ago, he decided to attack the problem. After getting permission from the local park board, Jim got to work.

First, he retrofitted a bicycle trailer into a sturdy cart to transport heavy gardening tools and haul away the weeds and debris. Then he committed up to four hours each day to digging, chopping, and towing the tree-sized weeds away. In addition to removing the buckthorn, Jim picks up garbage, cleans up goose droppings, and clears away milfoil, an invasive water weed that washes up on the lakeshore. In one year alone, he logged over 440 hours working at his waterside improvement project, which he views as his part-time job.

When asked about his work, Jim says modestly, "Oh, I don't know that I'm that interesting." But grateful neighbors and lake walkers have been interested and amazed to see Jim out in the snow, rain, and baking sun, quietly making the path along the creek and lake just a little bit prettier. Jim adds, "You don't need to go far to make a difference. You can clean up your alley or the street by your house. It all helps."

TRY THIS

Make a difference in your neighborhood. Start by taking a walk and picking up litter along the way, or choose a block near your home and dedicate time to keeping it clean. For a bigger commitment, check with your local park board, community garden, or Department of Natural Resources to find volunteer opportunities.

21

Faith on the Move
Jim and Norma, 80 years and 70 years

Jim and Norma have served people in need for decades through their four-hundred-person faith community. They took the commitment to a deeper level by selling their house and moving into a thousand-square-foot apartment in the low-income neighborhood their church has been supporting. A dozen other people from their faith community live in the same building. Now, Jim and Norma's retirement life is rich with daily outreach work.

One of their first projects was creating free, weeklong summer camps for kids in the neighborhood. Jim and Norma walked door to door, introducing themselves and getting to know the parents. When the camps opened, they were thrilled that fifty kids showed up. High school students from their church helped every day with crafts, games, and fun. "Parents responded so positively to the camps that they asked if we could do more," says Norma. In response, the couple started biweekly camps in the fall. About fifteen kids come for crafts, food, face painting, and acting out playful versions of Bible stories, such as falling down like the walls of Jericho.

Jim and Norma also provide outreach and support to an assisted-living and rehab center in the neighborhood. On Tuesdays they bring a group out for lunch. On Wednesdays and Thursdays they lead men's and women's groups. To connect even more with the residents at the center and with neighborhood families they serve through the camps, Jim and Norma bought a season pass for unlimited rides on a paddleboat that travels up and down the Mississippi River. They have used it many times throughout the summer. The ninety-minute adventure provided the opportunity to really get to know people and gave kids an exciting new experience. "Because we've gotten to see people often, we've really built friendships in the community," says Jim.

Jim and Norma find their untraditional living situation freeing and peaceful. "What you see is what we own," says Jim with a contented smile. The simplicity leaves them free to be on the move, serving their community, connecting with family, and living their faith. "We don't have many things," Jim adds, "but we have great relationships."

TRY THIS

Which neighborhood in your town needs the most support? Write down which of your talents you'd like to use to keep moving as you help out: home repair, gardening, playing with kids, or something else? Now check with area nonprofits or places of worship in that area to see how you can get moving and get involved.

MOVING WITH HEALTH LIMITATIONS

22

Time My Race with a Calendar
Carter, 70 years

Carter started running long before it was popular. "People would say, 'Why are you running around in your underwear?!'" he says, laughing. He ran between six and fifteen miles every day for decades, making a game of traversing every street and block in his city. He gave all his running routes simple titles based on landmarks, like "fire station run" or "four-store-corner run." Running defined him. When he wasn't working, he was running. Eventually, he began competing in state and national track meets and enjoyed great success. His fireplace mantel became a showcase crowded with ribbons, medals, and trophies.

When Carter was fifty-seven, he qualified for the World Masters track meet in Paris. He had dreamed of going to Paris since his college days, when he had earned a two-year degree in French. But, one month before the competition, Carter suffered a massive heart attack during a training session. He was training alone, so he wasn't found for some time. The lack of oxygen to his brain permanently affected his speech and balance. He spent two months in the hospital and a year in outpatient therapy. "It was a looong, laborious process," Carter explains. "At first I couldn't even walk with a walker. I had to relearn how to swallow food and tie my shoes. It was awful! But I kept on plugging away. I don't like it, but I keep going."

Now Carter can tie his shoes and walk slowly with a walker. With these milestones, he was able to return to the track, and he now participates in every indoor and outdoor track meet for athletes with disabilities that he can. With his trademark humor, Carter says, "Even the worst runner could slaughter me with this walker. So, I say to the timer, 'Don't use a stopwatch on me. Get out your calendar!'" Carter belts out a huge belly laugh and then adds with a sly smile, "But often there's no one in my division, so I get all the gold medals!"

TRY THIS

You don't have to be a competitive athlete to participate in sports. Research adaptive options for your favorite sport. Golf, volleyball, skiing, swimming, horseback riding, yoga, and tennis are just a few of the sports that can be adapted to accommodate physical limitations. Now ask yourself with kindness: are the limitations in your body or in your mind? Journal about all the things you can do. Then make a plan to begin.

23
Dog Park for Fitness and Friendship
Bill and Anne, 90 years and 56 years

Anne and Bill met while she was selling business textbooks to college professors and he was teaching at UCLA. Bill's handlebar moustache and effervescent personality attracted her right away. Anne's dry humor and love of outdoor adventure captured Bill's attention. Despite their big age difference, they fell deeply in love.

Where some saw an unlikely match, their friends and close family have seen decades of unconditional love. Their first twenty years of marriage were packed with outdoor adventures: hiking, skiing, mountain biking, and playing with their two beloved dogs. Bill took summer teaching stints in France, Australia, and Morocco, so Anne joined him in thrilling international explorations as well.

Bill's memory began to slip in his early eighties. Over the next several years, his mental and physical abilities declined further, and the couple's sporting adventures declined with them. Yet, their desire to exercise and connect with others remained. Anne began bringing Bill and the dogs to the local dog park, a fenced green space with a walking path and shaded sitting areas. Here, Anne could power-walk a mile of laps around the park while Bill strolled, and the dogs frolicked. Since Anne was always in view, Bill felt safe and calm.

Before long, Anne and Bill formed friendships with the other dog-park regulars, who were always patient and kind with Bill's memory challenges. They got to know the names and personalities of the other dogs, swapping funny tales of dog shenanigans and sharing the pain when someone's dog was sick or had died.

For about an hour each day, Anne, Bill, and the dogs got their exercise and a chance to connect with their dog-loving friends. If the pair missed a day, the regulars always checked in to make sure they were okay. Thanks to a shared love of dogs, Anne and Bill could still get outdoors and enjoy supportive friendships.

TRY THIS

If you have a dog, look for a dog park in your city and see if there's a welcoming regular crowd. If not, take your dog for a brisk walk through your neighborhood, celebrating the fact that people who walk their dog exercise an average of thirty minutes per day, the recommended amount for healthy living.

24
Diabetes and a Song
Audrey, 76 years

The other singers in Audrey's community choir had no idea she was recovering from triple bypass surgery and living with lifelong diabetes. She just warmly welcomed everyone and casually mentioned that the device attached to her side helped her monitor her health. Audrey has lived with diabetes since she was twelve years old, nearly died at age fourteen from the disease, and developed heart disease in her early sixties, culminating in the triple bypass.

"Diabetes is a lifestyle issue," Audrey explains. "I have to pay close attention to my health, or I feel awful. It's also helpful to be aware of my limitations so I can forgive myself for not being able to do all I want to do." Over time, Audrey has learned to be very selective in choosing goals so she can use her energy for what's most important to her. "It's a matter of finding things I *can* do, so I don't feel cheated."

For nearly twenty years Audrey has sung in the community choir with her husband, Bob, even though she had no prior experience singing. The choir performs at nursing homes and care facilities several times each year, so Audrey has gotten a lot of practice. "I still don't feel really confident singing, but I do like trying. And the people in the choir have become our friends." A highlight for the group was performing at the wedding of a fellow choir member.

Audrey also takes care of her two grandchildren two or three times each week and attends their weekly sporting events when her energy allows. She also enjoys memoir writing and meeting with her friends, noting, "We always have something good to talk about!"

Audrey and Bob have worked to adapt to her health limitations. For example, Bob might walk for two hours to practice his photography while Audrey focuses on her writing. When the couple travels together, they choose destinations where trusted health care is available. Yet Bob also longs for rugged travel, so Audrey joyfully supported his five trips with Global Volunteers and Habitat for Humanity to help with hurricane relief efforts.

"I think it's really important to be accepting of others' needs," says Audrey. "Otherwise it gets a little strained and stressful."

TRY THIS

If you or your partner has health limitations, brainstorm a list of all the activities you can still do. Choose one this week and do it.

GET OUTSIDE

25
Woodburning Stove Workout
Don, 76 years

"Get yourself a woodburning stove." That's Don's advice for retirees who want to stay in shape but hate structured exercise. Don had a woodburning stove when he lived in Cincinnati in the 1970s, so he knew he liked it. So, early in retirement he installed a woodstove to heat his home in the country near Richmond, Indiana. The stove is a practical way to stay warm if the power goes out. "It's great built-in exercise," Don says. "It saves you money and certainly keeps your muscles toned up."

Every morning throughout the fall and winter, Don gets up before his wife and loads the stove. "By the time she's up for breakfast, the room's warm as toast." Every three or four hours he adds a few more logs. Don says it's not hard work to keep the house heated. You can leave the stove without adding wood for up to twenty-four hours and still get heat.

The stove helps Don keep moving in the spring and summer, too, because he chops all his own wood. The wood is easy to find; the emerald ash borer, an invasive insect, has killed all the ash trees in his area. He clears dead trees that his neighbors don't want on their land and uses them for firewood. Don figures he handles each tree about ten times between chopping, hand splitting, loading in his truck, hauling to the barn, and eventually stacking inside his house and loading into the stove.

Don loves working with the wood and how strong it makes him. "Reach over here and grab my arm," he says with warm pride. "You feel that?! I don't go to the gym, and I'm almost eighty years old. That woodstove is the greatest thing going!"

TRY THIS

Think about the type of manual labor that makes you feel strong and accomplished. It might be house painting, gardening, demolition, building, or something else. Choose a project that uses that strength, whether it's for your own home or for a nonprofit like Habitat for Humanity.

26

Wag More, Bark Less
Barry, 63 years

B arry helps dogs "wag more and bark less" through a variety of volunteer roles at his local Animal Humane Society. His tasks have ranged from helping with adoptions and dog walking to the time-consuming job of fostering dogs in his home.

When Barry brings dogs from the kennel to the visiting room and helps people find the right match for adoption, he feels hopeful. "It's great to see a happy family or older person get a dog—and to see a dog get a new life," he says. As a dog walker, he gets social time with the dogs as well as about two miles of exercise.

While shelters try to house every pet, they often lack the space or resources to provide proper care. This is particularly true for puppies that are too young or sick to spay or neuter. When Barry fosters puppies, he feeds, bathes, and plays with them. Of course, he does a lot of cleaning up after the little ones as he gets them used to people. He's also taken older dogs that are injured or sick and need time to heal before they're ready for adoption. He administers medicines or tends to wounds as needed, and he gets to know the personality of each animal to help families make the best forever home match.

Barry recalls fostering four puppies that had survived from a litter of eight sick siblings. For two weeks he nursed the fragile survivors back to health. "Once the puppies were healthy, I got to see them get adopted during my next couple volunteer shifts. One family even sent me a photo of the puppy doing well," Barry says. "Helping a person find the right match and then handing off the animal is my favorite thing." Without willing fosterers like Barry, more dogs would have to be euthanized. It's no exaggeration to say he's saving dogs' lives. Now that's a reason to wag more!

TRY THIS

Contact your area animal shelter to see how you can help. You can work directly with animals: grooming, socializing, and providing support at adoption events. If you want to use more brain than brawn, offer your work skills: legal aid, website support, medical services, or office support.

27

Healing in the Garden
Winnie, 73 years

Winnie's love of gardening helps her endure the pain of losing her son, Graham. "When you lose a child, even if they're an adult, they're always your little boy, so grief is a constant companion. But you go on and live because they can't."

Winnie chooses to carry on by spending time every day in her garden. The connection to nature soothes her, and the physical labor of digging, hauling, and planting is energizing and satisfying. "I love to plant something and then stand back and let it bless me. 'Cuz boy-oh-boy it's beautiful!" She also finds healing in helping neighbors with their gardens, suggesting what to plant and where to plant it. "I'm outside all the time in my garden, and that's how I meet people. One thing leads to another."

She remembers the very first week she moved to her town in Colorado. She was clearing out the garden beds when a woman stopped to admire her work. After chatting a bit, the woman told Winnie, "They say I have a brain tumor." From then on, she stopped by Winnie's garden every day for a year just to chat. The woman had lived in that small town for years and probably had hundreds of friends, but she came to visit because Winnie was digging in the dirt and planting pretty things, and because Winnie could relate to her pain.

"I was so honored that she started that conversation, even though she was so ill with chemo and had no hair," Winnie says. "Sometimes acquaintances are easier to be with in times of grief than friends. You don't have their backstory. You're not dwelling on 'how's so-and-so doing,' it's just right there."

The pain of losing her son has been unspeakable, but Winnie has carried her experience of grieving into the garden to strengthen her body and heal her heart. People have been stopping by ever since.

TRY THIS

For many people, it's easier to share their thoughts while moving. Choose one safe friend or family member with whom you'd like to practice really listening. Invite them for coffee, a walk, a round of golf, or to shoot hoops. When they're talking, give them your full attention. Hold back from jumping in with your story. Instead, ask at least three questions about their story to show your genuine interest in them.

UNTRADITIONAL TRAVEL

28

Wilderness Guide to Peace and Friendship
Kath, 67 years

The wilderness is where Kath finds peace, empowerment, and friendship. Growing up with an alcoholic, abusive father, she often took refuge in the woods around her home. When, as a young adult, she came out as a lesbian, she was afraid she'd be kicked out of her family, so she sought out strength and healing in the wilderness.

Today she continues her adventures with the self-named Sturdy Girls group. Kath and her three friends have been exploring the outdoors together for over forty years. Sometimes they take day trips to hike or bike. They've also volunteered as dog runners for the John Beargrease Sled Dog Marathon in northern Minnesota. Once a year they plan an extended camping trip with just their compasses, the stars, the animals, and each other. "We have great conversations. And we gently push each other to take the action we need in life. It's very healing," says Kath. "The wilderness is our spirituality. Our time outdoors provides a satisfying mental, physical, and spiritual challenge."

For thirty years Kath has also led wilderness adventure trips for people of all abilities throughout North America, working her schedule around her day job as an accountant. One week she might be guiding able-bodied people hiking segments of the 310-mile Superior Hiking Trail along Lake Superior and another she might be taking a group of paraplegic people whitewater rafting in the Grand Canyon. Kath particularly loves guiding groups of women. "There's a strength that women have in communicating with each other and in empowering each person to do their best, whatever that is."

Kath recalls a kayak trip she guided for twelve women. Some had never camped, and one used a wheelchair. The group faced a quarter-mile trek from the water to their campsite that required hauling their six boats, gear, and food. For three hours they worked together to transport their kayaks and supplies, with the woman in the wheelchair taking the lead to guide the others over rough terrain. "By the end of the day, the bond between the women was so strong after figuring out how to work together so well," says Kath. "I feel like I'm making a difference. I'm making an impact on people's lives, and they on me."

Not all of Kath's trips are so intense. Her partner, Nancy, enjoys the outdoors but in a less hard-core way. "We bought a little camper so we can travel in a way that's comfortable for both of us." Both avid bikers, they bring their bikes along and explore the back roads together. Whether she's roughing it in remote areas or enjoying the ease of a camper, Kath finds peace, connection, and movement in the outdoors.

TRY THIS

To get a tiny taste of peace in the wilderness, try shinrin-yoku, the Japanese practice of forest bathing. It takes four simple steps: 1. Leave your phone behind. 2. Leave your goals behind. 3. Wander in nature, noticing the small beauties. 4. Sit quietly, and soak in the stillness. Studies show that after just fifteen minutes of forest bathing, blood pressure drops, stress is reduced, and concentration improves. Imagine what a whole weekend in the woods could do!

29
Faith-Fueled Travel
Sally and Elgin, 77 years

Sally and Elgin's faith-fueled adventures have kept their bodies moving, their minds awake, and their hearts open.

Their travels began with their four grandchildren. When each grandchild turned fourteen or fifteen, Sally and Elgin took them on an intergenerational mission trip to Peru, sponsored by their church. For a week they joined other family teams to teach English, share crafts, play games, and build intercultural understanding. Each trip presented obstacles that could have affected their experience, but, as Sally says, "God always provided." For example, when their granddaughter Abby took the trip, there were no girls on the team her age. Instead of feeling left out, she used the international language of soccer to connect with a local girl, Fatima, on the playground. Their friendship grew quickly, and when it came time to say goodbye, Abby gave Fatima her favorite pro soccer jersey.

A couple of years before retiring, Elgin began thinking about how to stay engaged in his postcareer life. On a whim, he submitted a volunteer application with the United States Agency for International Development (USAID), a governmental organization that leads international development and humanitarian aid. Elgin's experience as an ad executive was a long shot for the typical USAID roles, which focus on agriculture, health, and the environment, so he figured he would never hear back. However, an ad agency in Kazakhstan needed Elgin's skills to strengthen its business strategy. Sally was up for the adventure, offering her upbeat attitude that "Sure, we can do this if God is calling us there!"

For eight weeks, Sally and Elgin lived in Ust, Kazakhstan, navigating a foreign language, unfamiliar foods, and unknown cultural norms. Elgin worked daily at the ad agency, sharing insights on marketing issues and client relationship building. He met with all of the agency's clients, listened to their business problems, and worked with them to find solutions. Meanwhile, Sally's bubbly personality attracted a word-of-mouth group of "students" to practice English. They gathered to talk, laugh, and joke around, all in English, while Sally helped with pronunciation. They fell in love with Sally and threw her a big party when the time came for them to leave. "The world felt smaller once we experienced life halfway around the world," says Elgin. "There are good people everywhere. We left a bit of our hearts in Kazakhstan."

That experience led Sally and Elgin to follow another call for faith-filled travel, this time for six months in Niger, West Africa. "The Niger trip fell in our laps. We felt called, even though we had no idea what we were doing and were out of our skill area," explains Elgin. The original plan was to help run a modest retreat center where employees doing field work in the area could take a break and reenergize. When Sally and Elgin arrived ready to work, however, they found a huge problem: the local people didn't want them there.

Sally and Elgin decided to let go of their assigned roles and look for other ways to contribute to the community. Sally got involved with the local people, earning their trust and making friends. She says, "There were times I thought, 'I don't know if I can do this for six months!' Then some opportunity to help out would appear, and that gave me energy and joy." Elgin found simple, useful jobs like cleaning out a shed or organizing materials. He discovered it was unexpectedly energizing. "I had just retired and went from being kinda a big deal to not being in charge of anything. I learned how satisfying it can be to help however I can. It was fantastic!" Through kindness and a genuine commitment to contributing in whatever way was most helpful, they became a welcome addition to the community. "We learned an awful lot about ourselves," Elgin recalls. "We learned that it can be enough just to be present with others and that getting out of our comfort zone can be a real upper! You do whatever comes around."

Sally adds, "Many people are so afraid they won't have something to do in retirement. I say, 'Don't be afraid, it's exciting! There are more opportunities out there than you can count.'"

TRY THIS

There are many international service roles for older adults that cover the costs of travel, food, and lodging in exchange for service work. Searching "international service" or "global volunteers" brings up many organizations like the International Executive Service Corps (IESC), the Peace Corps, and Global Volunteers. Try a weeklong service, and you might be inspired to go for a year!

30

Road Tripping for Adventure and Antiques
Dave, 76 years

After being retired for twenty-one years, Dave and his wife, Carla, like to get away from each other for a few days and then meet up in a new city for a simple vacation. The couple chooses a destination and the date they'll reunite. Then Dave gets in his red pickup truck and drives across the country by himself. Carla flies to meet him later.

"Carla likes Vegas the best, but we've met up in San Francisco, San Diego, Portland, and Seattle—pretty much every big city in the West," Dave explains. "It isn't elaborate, but we can afford a plane ticket and a hotel for a week. It's a great vacation." Plus, he likes to drive, and she doesn't. "I wouldn't want her with me anyway," Dave laughs. "This way I'm the boss the whole time, and I can win all my arguments along the way."

As he travels, Dave likes to stop at historic markers to get to know a place. He remembers one roadside stop where the wagon wheel paths of the Oregon Trail were still visible. "There I was, looking at the wheel tracks," recalls Dave. "I was thinking of those people caravanning across the country, while my pickup engine idled, keeping my car warm."

A guiding force of these driving adventures is Dave's passion for antiques. Before he hits the road, Dave maps out antique sales and flea markets to check out good deals.

He looks for beat-up pieces that have been used and abused and wound up in a barn or basement.

When Dave finds something he likes, he brings it back to the workshop in his barn and carefully restores it so someone else can enjoy and use it for the next hundred years. "I've filled my house with them and all my kids' houses with them. So now I give the antiques to charity, and they auction them off like crazy so they can earn some money. That keeps me having fun."

Dave shares a passion for antiques with Richard Petty, a retired NASCAR star of the 1970s. He's proud to say that eight of his pieces are now in Petty's boyhood home, which is now a museum. While Dave's red truck isn't a race car, it has carried him through a lot of satisfying road-trip adventures.

TRY THIS

Plan a day trip in your area. Use the same curiosity you'd give to planning an international adventure. Tour the quirky attractions. Sample local restaurants, shops, and breweries. Search out new trails for biking or hiking. See if you're inspired to plan longer adventures.

CONNECT WITH OTHERS

Who You Gonna Call?

Be patient with your friendships.
—Mary, 85 years

Friendships and family dynamics aren't the most natural thing in the world. You have to work at them. Put your flaws out there and be open.
—Warren, 77 years

Nothing is more important than investing time and energy in the relationships in our lives, even though they might drive us a little crazy. When relationships end or fade, we can muster the courage to cultivate new ones. Think of all the times ahead when you may want a lunch buddy, a travel companion, or a helping hand during a tough time. With a nod to the movie *Ghostbusters*, ask yourself, "Who you gonna call?!"

Research on the importance of maintaining close relationships is compelling and even shocking. "Loneliness kills," states Robert Waldinger, director of the Harvard Study of Adult Development, one of the longest studies on adult life. "It's as powerful as smoking and alcoholism."[6]

The people I spoke with who had relatives nearby had a head start. Even though families can be messy, they stayed connected through everything from sharing simple birthday dinners to attending grandkids' sporting events, caregiving, and planning showstopping activities. Those who were distant from or had lost ties with their family figured out how to develop meaningful relationships from scratch. They spoke passionately about how important it has been to step outside their comfort zones and work on developing relationships. Though this didn't come easily to many of the people I interviewed, they chose to do *something* to connect with others, whether it was joining an organization, pursuing a passion, or opening their hearts to the neighbors around them.

Spending all those bonus retirement hours with a spouse or significant other, however, can challenge your relationship, especially if you don't plan for meaningful time apart. There's a saying gaining in popularity: "I married for life, not for lunch." If one person in a couple expects the other to provide all the social support, tension is bound to develop. Many couples face serious stress when they don't discuss how to balance time together and apart.

---

[6] Liz Mineo, "Good Genes Are Nice, but Joy Is Better," *Harvard Gazette*, April 11, 2017, https://news.harvard.edu/gazette/story/2017/04/over-nearly-80-years-harvard-study-has-been-showing-how-to-live-a-healthy-and-happy-life.

The following stories introduce people doing the hard work of maintaining ongoing relationships and bravely developing new ones, and of couples working together and apart. We all need companions along the way, so let's figure out "Who you gonna call?"

WON'T YOU BE MY NEIGHBOR?

31

Neighbors, Friends, and Hockey Lovers
Warren and Logan, 77 years and 7 years

Next-door neighbors Warren and Logan forged a deep friendship thanks to their love of hockey. It all started when Logan was four years old and Warren was in his early seventies. If Warren's garage door was open, that meant he was probably outside, so Logan would pop over, hockey stick in hand, to talk about a recent game while practicing his stick handling. If Logan was outside, whacking a ball around, Warren might wander over to coach him on his shot and talk hockey stats.

When Logan learned that Warren played hockey four times a week with a group of men, he begged his mom to let him play with the "old guys' team." For two years while Logan was in preschool, his mom laced up his skates twice a week to play with the "old guys." The men loved shooting the puck around with Logan and were always disappointed when he couldn't make it. When Logan started kindergarten, he and Warren set a standing date to skate on days off from school. As time went on, the two friends attended college hockey games together, wearing matching baseball hats and scheming about Logan playing for Notre Dame someday.

When asked how this friendship began, Warren got misty-eyed, recalling, "When my wife was dying, Logan's mom organized the whole neighborhood to bring meals to us. She'd bring Logan over with the meals. And that little boy, I tell you, he *knew* he was doing good. He'd come in and cheer up my wife and me. To see someone that young trying to comfort a sixty-six-year-old lady . . . and then watch him march down the driveway with such purpose because he knew he'd done good. Now, I ask you, how can you *not* fall in love with a little boy like that?!"

Since Warren's grandkids live out of town and Logan's grandpa also lives far away, their friendship blossomed into a sort of bonus grandpa/grandson relationship. Logan invited Warren to his preschool's Grandparents/Special Person Program, and, when he spotted Warren in the audience, he lit up and gave him a wave and a thumbs-up. At the cookies-and-juice reception afterward, Logan showed Warren his classroom and artwork. His grandparents were there too, but Warren was truly Logan's special guest.

TRY THIS

If you don't know your neighbors, revive the old tradition of offering neighborly gifts, and bring over a home-cooked treat or offer a plant from your yard. Start a conversation to see if you share an interest like cooking, baking, books, or home repair.

32
Cell Phone Connection
Lois, 100 years

Lois's cell phone has been her lifeline to maintaining great connections in her later years. After her husband died, Lois chose to move from their lifelong home into a senior residence nearby, spending winters with her daughter and son-in-law in Florida. She loved her years in this new home, where she developed and deepened new friendships.

This arrangement worked well, for five years, but then Lois took a fall and also had kidney failure. Her kids told her she needed to move to Florida full-time to be near her daughter. "My heart just fell down into my shoes at that," says Lois, "but I'd known people for years who'd tried to get their parents to do something for their own good and everyone got mad. So, I just thought, 'Lois, you can't go there. You've just got to think positive about moving.'" And that's just what she did.

Lois now lives in Fort Myers, Florida, in an assisted-living apartment complex where she plays bingo three times a week, does yoga twice a week, and attends a Tuesday church service. Most weekends she spends at her daughter's home on nearby Captiva Island. Lois's daughter invited her to move in with her, but Lois wants to keep up her social life without burdening her daughter with driving.

In addition to her new connections in Florida, Lois keeps up with family members and friends across the country using her cell phone. She talks with her three sons every week. Her oldest son calls every day at 4:30 p.m., her second son calls every Sunday afternoon, and her third son calls several times a week while he's traveling for work. Lois's cousin checks in every evening at 8:15 for a daily chat, and a friend from Missouri calls on Tuesday afternoons for a visit.

Some of the calls slowly fell into a pattern, while others were set up intentionally. Lois explains, "My forty-six-year-old grandson, Jud, said to me, 'Grammy, I'm going to call you every Monday at 8:30 p.m. if you'd like that.' And I said, 'Oh, I'd *love* that!' And oh boy! He doesn't miss!" Lois continues, "Jud said to me, 'Well, I usually know what everybody's doing and have tidbits of information, so we won't have a hard time talking for thirty minutes.'"

Lois also loves to keep in touch with faraway friends. She uses the directory and newsletter from her first senior residence to keep track of birthdays. "I call everyone on their birthdays around breakfast time and sing Happy Birthday," Lois says through a ripple of laughter. "They'll always say, 'Oh, you're the first one who called!' You just *have* to call first thing or the day slips away." Lois never lets a day slip away without connecting with someone she loves, thanks to her cell phone.

TRY THIS

All of us long for connection, but most of us are hesitant to be the first one to reach out. Dare to make the first move. List five people you've been meaning to reconnect with and send a text or email or pick up the phone and say hello. If it goes well, ask if they'd like to chat again sometime. Then, set a time and check in again.

33

If You Scoop It, They Will Come
Norma and Jim, 70 years and 80 years

Norma and Jim live in a typical middle-class suburb with attached garages and no sidewalks. People can come and go without ever seeing their neighbors. When they retired, they decided to put a wraparound front porch on their home to try to connect with their neighbors. The couple enjoyed sitting out front on the inviting chairs or the porch swing, greeting people as they strolled by. Jim, a cheerful extrovert, dubbed himself the mayor of their area and even bought bunting for the railing.

Neighbors commented about what a lovely porch they had. Norma says, "I'd always say, 'C'mon up and sit down for a while.' But they'd always say, 'Oh, no, thanks.'" To encourage people to accept that invitation, Norma and Jim created a neighborhood event. Several times each summer they'd put flyers up throughout the area and post a sign on their porch: "Meet Your Neighbors at the Free Root Beer Float Party!"

The first year about twenty people showed up. As the years went on, it grew to more than a hundred people gathering for floats and a chance to connect. Norma and Jim loved seeing people make new friends or connect with old ones. They'd hear people exclaim, "Oh, I haven't seen you since our kids graduated twenty years ago!" One time, two women who worked in the same business discovered they lived just blocks apart.

"The root beer float parties kind of made us known in the neighborhood," Norma shares. "We didn't feel much connection until we did this, and it really helped us get to know people." Jim stresses that you don't need a porch to try this idea. "You can host a gathering in your garage or yard. And it doesn't cost a fortune. Do you know we fed 125 people root beer floats for just forty dollars?! Norma is great at finding the deals."

TRY THIS

Host your own neighborhood gathering. Start by inviting just the people on your block or the floor of your apartment building. Try any of the following themes: cookie exchange, chili contest, appetizer potluck, beer tasting, pumpkin-carving contest, or bike parade for kids and adults. Consider encouraging participation by offering prizes for best flavor, most creative, most outrageous, and so on.

GRANDPARENTING

34
Cousins' Camp
Jane and Odin, 77 years

Jane and Odin love spending time with their four grandkids throughout the year, going to activities, sharing meals, and celebrating holidays. When the kids were little, they wanted to create an annual event that would "knock the socks off" the grandkids, so they dreamed up Cousins' Camp.

All year long the couple had fun brainstorming adventures, crafts, and games for the camp. Jane and Odin also designed a closing presentation for the kids' parents. When it was finally time for Cousins' Camp, Jane and Odin gathered the grandkids in the city where they all live and then traveled with the whole gang to their cabin for the weekend festivities.

Each year Cousins' Camp featured a special theme. During an election year, the theme was "Presidents." The group visited candidates at the state fair, worked on a giant puzzle of all the US presidents, and learned a song about the presidents to perform for their parents at the end of the weekend. "Mark Twain" was the inspiration another year. After reading stories about Tom Sawyer and Huck Finn, the four grandkids worked together to build a simple wooden raft just like Huck's. The raft proved seaworthy, so everyone took a turn paddling it out onto the nearby lake. One year, with "King Tut" as the theme, Jane and Odin greeted the kids in pharaoh costumes and brought them to an Egyptian exhibit before heading to the cabin. Over the weekend, the kids had fun with Egyptian-inspired activities like learning about hieroglyphics and decorating shoebox "tombs" for Barbie dolls. The closing presentation included a performance of a song about pharaohs, a mysterious hieroglyphic code that the parents had to decipher, and a contest to see who could mummify their dad in toilet paper the fastest.

Ten years of memory making through "knock your socks off" adventures have given Jane and Odin a priceless connection with their grandkids and created a special bond among the cousins. This warm affection extends to Jane and Odin's adult children, who feel grateful for the magic created at Cousins' Camp.

TRY THIS

Plan a one time grandkids' event. Explore your town like tourists, let each kid choose an adventure, or simply host a movie night. Just give it a test run and see what works.

35
Just Show Up
Jim S., 83 years

Jim played baseball all his life, so following his grand-kids' soccer games was new territory for him. He genuinely enjoyed going to games every week, though, because he wasn't there to follow a team: he was there to be a part of his grandkids' lives.

At the start of each season, Jim got the game schedule from his daughter-in-law and then showed up at as many games as he could. The memories from those games ignite Jim. "Once, when my grandson, Chase, was pretty young, he was back almost to midfield. The goalie was too far out, so Chase looped one over his head and scored. Oh man! Chase looked over his shoulder and did a little dance. It just knocked us all over," Jim recalls. "And my grand-daughter, Hannah, also launched one from midfield, scored, and turned to look for us—and the jubilance! I'll remember that forever."

Since his son and daughter-in-law worked full-time, Jim also offered to help carpool. That simple offer would bring long-lasting gratitude from any overscheduled parent, but Jim says, "It was no chore to drive the kids. It was a pleasure to have the bonding time with them." And Jim realized talking or emailing with their parents two or three times each week to coordinate schedules had a hidden benefit. "Being so involved with my grandkids not only built a bond with my grandkids, it helped solidify my relationship with my son and his wife. It gave us things to talk about, helped make us closer, and prevented us from drifting apart as can happen with other families."

TRY THIS

If your grandkids live nearby, choose one of their events to check out. If they live far away, ask to watch a game through FaceTime or Skype, or schedule a call to recap the event highlights.

36
Pizza with a Side of Love
Joy, 80 years

"I get a big bang out of affirming people in their unique-ness," says Joy, "because I experienced the opposite." Joy is a bold survivor of an abusive marriage. She left it with no job skills and three young children, including one with special needs. Fortunately, Joy also left with an abundance of faith. That faith gave her healing and led her to jobs and relationships that would fulfill her for the next thirty-three years.

Today, Joy loves to lift others up, starting with her five grandkids. She takes each of them to lunch alone to celebrate birthdays or other special occasions. Sometimes they go to an evening church service and out to dinner. Joy also attends as many of their games and activities as she can. "At one point, all five kids were playing hockey, so I had quite a schedule," laughs Joy.

As the older grandkids headed off to college, Joy has stayed in touch by email. "They know I'm not a 'techie' grandma, so they're good about responding with emails," Joy says. "I tell them I don't expect to hear from them with every email. But they're dear about keeping in touch."

Joy confesses that she's not a cooking and baking grandma, but she can deliver a hot pizza. One time, when her daughter's flight got delayed, Joy brought a pizza dinner over to the younger kids and spent the evening with them. Her fourteen-year-old grandson sent a thank-you note reading, "Hey, Grandma, I just wanted to say thank you for the pizza tonight. I really appreciate your generosity and don't thank you enough. You're the best grandmother a grandson could ask for." After sharing that story, Joy paused to wipe her tears and then said, "No amount of money is better than that! This is where it's at for me."

Of course, her grandson's gratitude isn't really about the pizza. It's about how Joy expresses her love and acceptance when she's with her grandkids. She makes a point of telling each grandkid, "I'm proud of what you *do*. But I love you for *who you are*! You don't have to prove anything to me."

Joy also encourages them to take time for their spiritual growth. She says, "You get to be my age, and you find faith is where it's at. It doesn't matter a hill of beans if you're a millionaire. What matters is who you are. Do what Saint Francis de Sales said: 'Be who you are, and be that well.'"

TRY THIS

Create a simple, standing date with each grandchild. Ideally, get together in person for a meal or shared activity. If you don't live within driving distance, establish a regular time to connect through technology. Many grandparents have discovered the joy of using Zoom, Skype, or other platforms to play Pictionary, charades, Jeopardy!, and other classic favorites with their families.

CREATE BONDS
THROUGH SERVICE

37

Cuban Connections
Doris, 65 years

Doris was grateful to the church she grew up in because it had an active outreach program welcoming Chinese immigrant families like her own. After being away for twenty years, she returned to the church to raise her daughter there and to find volunteer roles that could help her give back. That volunteer structure was just what she needed when her husband died unexpectedly in his early sixties.

"You never think it's going to happen to you. But it was only six months, and he was gone," explains Doris. "I decided to live by the mantra that you have to do what you can, when you can, because you never know what's going to happen." To live out her mantra, Doris decided to travel, for fun and for service.

"Right after my husband died, I took my daughter on her first service trip to Cuba. She'd just graduated from college, and the trip sparked a long commitment to all things Cuban." Doris's church has had a partnership with a church in Cuba for nearly twenty years, providing services such as installing water filtration systems in local communities. "The government laid the sewer pipes and freshwater pipes in the same trenches," explains Doris. "For the government to dig them up, well, that'll never happen." Thus, the installation of clean-water systems is vital to community safety.

Doris's group raises funds for the systems and trains volunteers on the installation process and educational outreach. Doris trains the educators to help locals prioritize use of the filtered water for drinking and for bathing children. The unfiltered water is fine for washing clothes, dishes, and adults.

Typically, the volunteers install the clean-water systems in churches, which provide clean water as a service to the community. In a recent trip, however, the city requested that they install a system in a government-run cooking school so more residents could get access to clean water. This change was surprising because the government had acknowledged the problem with municipal water.

Connecting with volunteers and locals energizes Doris. "This work has been really rewarding," she says. "There's a particular area where we've really gotten to know the people, even though I'm not fluent in Spanish. Their culture is very loving, filled with hugging. I just love it."

TRY THIS

If international service work entices you, research service organizations that are dedicated to positively engaging the local community. Or join a group in your area that's committed to international service.

38

Finding a Friendship Match
Kate, 67 years

Retirement hit Kate hard. After working at the same company for forty-two years, she was laid off and forced into early retirement. After that earth-shaking shock, she granted herself permission to "just be" for a while. Then Kate started sampling classes and volunteer roles. She tried tai chi and hated it. She volunteered in hospice and had a good experience, but it wasn't what she was looking for. "I found you have to get past the feeling that you failed if a class or volunteer role isn't a fit," she told me. "Just keep trying things."

After exploring options for a couple of years, Kate saw a newspaper ad from a Boston nonprofit that matches volunteers with homebound older adults for weekly visits based on the volunteer's schedule. Kate got matched with 102-year-old Henrietta. During their weekly visits, Henrietta slowly shared fragments of her life history.

Her fascinating story starts in South Carolina, where she was raised by her great-grandmother, a powerful figure for the family because she was freed from slavery at age four. In the 1920s, her great-grandmother moved Henrietta and the whole family to Boston. "Boston wasn't a very friendly place at that time if you were Black—still isn't so great," says Kate. "Henrietta doesn't tell a lot of stories about the negative things. But because I know Boston's history, I can ask her questions about that time.

She's been telling me about the jobs she had and about her kids. Each bit of her life that Henrietta shares is a gift to me. I really appreciate that."

Henrietta also tells Kate about the importance of going to church and singing in the choir. "She hasn't been able to go to church and sing for a very long time due to her health. So I said, 'You know, I can get music on my phone. If there's a song you'd like, just let me know.' When I found her favorite song and lyrics on YouTube, Henrietta took the phone and just read and sang." Remembering the moment, Kate says through joyful tears, "Henrietta had the face of pure bliss! She was just so happy! It was so amazing! Every week Henrietta exclaims, 'Oh, I'm just so glad you come to see me!'" Kate has come to realize she's so happy she came, too. She finally found her match.

TRY THIS

To find your service match, think about what age range appeals to you. Older adults? Teens? Grade school or younger? Many national organizations need volunteer mentors, buddies, and friends who can connect in person or virtually. Try United Way, Big Brothers/Big Sisters, Foster Grandparents, or a social service agency near you.

39
One Cause, Different Roles
Connie and Jack, 79 years

Connie and Jack's commitment to their church is the foundation of their lives. To live out their faith, they have both committed countless hours throughout their marriage to nonprofit organizations and church communities. While the work was wonderful, they found that the balance between volunteering and sharing time together was out of whack. "We realized we were both running around like crazy, and this wasn't good or healthy for our marriage," explains Jack. "So, we made the decision that from here on out, the things we volunteer to do, we do together."

They chose several organizations in which they both found meaningful roles that matched their skills and interests. Jack might be on the finance committee at their church while Connie helps lead the church's retreats or faith formation. "We've been on about a gazillion committees at church," laughs Jack. "This way, we could go to all the social events together and share mutual friends."

Their longest and strongest commitment has been to volunteer work in Haiti. The founder of a small nonprofit called Mission Haiti spoke at their church. As a nurse, Connie felt such an urgent call to go that she told Jack she was going with or without him. Jack chuckles affectionately while remembering his first reaction to Connie's commitment. "I thought, 'Oh, I don't know about this. The challenges stink to high heaven. But Connie's heart is in this, so I'm screwed! I'm going to Haiti too.'"

In the eighteen years since, the couple has traveled to Haiti with the organization up to three times each year. Jack, Connie, and the Mission Haiti team have helped the local Catholic nuns grow their parish services from a four-room elementary school to providing a primary school, support for university education, a culinary trade school, eldercare, and a sustainable farming operation. "We really believe the only way out of poverty in Haiti is through education," says Connie.

While they love their work in Haiti, the travel is physically demanding. In the past few years, Jack has faced significant health challenges, including balance issues and neuropathy in his upper body. So, he made the hard choice to take his last trip. Seven family members joined Jack and Connie to share in the power of the gifts they've given and relationships with their Haitian friends. Staying true to their commitment, Jack continues to support Mission Haiti from home while Connie plans to travel a bit longer, while her health allows.

TRY THIS

To discover a service area that you and a loved one can share, independently make lists of ten issues that interest each of you. Then list ten organizations that you've each always been curious about. Compare lists and find the connections. Get creative about how your shared interests can serve a local organization.

JOIN A GROUP OR CREATE A CLUB

40
Master Club Member
Joan, 83 years

One of the easiest ways to develop new friendships is joining an existing club. Joan is a master club member. After losing her husband, she found that having weekly or monthly standing activities kept her engaged with people of different ages and interests. Joan is in a monthly wine club, book club, garden club, birthday club, and golf league. "I'm a rotten golfer," Joan confesses, "but if I take a weekly lesson, then I get to play the course with others, so that works out."

One of the newest additions to Joan's weekly activities is her "salon," a discussion group that follows a video series called The Great Courses. The hosts of the salon, a husband-wife duo, invested in the full set of DVDs, which offer college-level courses on topics ranging from music and science to travel and philosophy. The couple thought the series would be fun to do in a group, and so the salon was born.

Each week the group chooses two videos. They watch the first thirty-minute video and then discuss it for thirty minutes. After a short break for treats, they repeat the process with a second video. When we met, the group had just focused on classic novels such as *Wuthering Heights* by Emily Brontë, and *Moby Dick* by Herman Melville. "During discussions, there can be divergent opinions or agreement. Often we note in just plain amazement how rich a novel can be, and all that we may have missed in the past when we 'needed' to read it for school!" Joan explains. "There is full realization that our life experiences bring a rich body of knowledge that most often was lacking in our late teens and college years."

Joan didn't really know the salon members when she was invited to join, but is thrilled to be making new friends and learning new things too. "Each of us comes with an open mind, but we truly are products of our family backgrounds and values. It is quite fascinating to just observe how the discussions evolve." Joan adds, "You know, it's so easy to do a salon. The guests don't have to prepare anything in advance. We just gather round the TV and go. And the host keeps it really simple. She just has a pot of coffee and some cookies, that's it. It wouldn't be too difficult for a curious-minded person to start a salon, and I would heartily encourage them to do so."

TRY THIS

There are numerous online learning options, and many are free. Check out Coursera.org, a website that partners with universities worldwide to provide free online learning. Explore TED Talks or YouTube videos. Then, try a one time salon. Simply invite two people and ask each of them to bring a friend or two. Boot up your computer and go. If your group prefers, salons can easily take place on Zoom, Skype, or Facebook Group Call.

41
Friendly Philosophers Group
Gib, 68 years

Philosophy always appealed to Gib. As a rebellious, deep-thinking self-described hippie in the 1960s, he used philosophy to wrestle through recovery from drug abuse, divorce, and even a nervous breakdown at age twenty-two. The breakdown terrified him. He decided he needed to do whatever he needed to take care of his mental health. "I was a radical wild-ass with a big commitment to 'fix the world.' Philosophy helped me answer important questions in life. Therapy helped heal a lot. The Christ thing always made sense to me too, even though I railed against God all the time. This combination of beliefs gave meaning to my life."

After retiring from his day job as an airline reservations agent, Gib channeled his passion for philosophical thinking by founding the Friendly Philosophers Group, one part of a small nonprofit he created to build community and raise the level of enlightenment in the world. This informal group meets weekly in the community room of Gib's apartment complex to discuss the "inner workings of faith, ethics, and science." Using the online app Nextdoor.com and the website Meetup.com to invite participation, Gib gathered members of wide-ranging disciplines and schools of thought. The group includes teachers, writers, photographers, and scientists. Their beliefs range from devout Christians to atheists.

Each week Gib introduces a different theme to get the free-flowing conversation going. There is no assigned reading or advance study; members are just asked to come with a curious, open mind to share their thoughts on the topic of the week. Past themes have ranged from science-focused questions, such as "The earth is unraveling due to human-forced warming—true or false?" to personal belief inquiries like "What course changes have you made in your belief system recently?" and politically influenced topics like "A discussion of fake news, starting with the famous 1994 legal case against McDonald's." Gib believes that "providing a space for our various perspectives inspires an invigorated commitment to social, political, and environmental justice."

"The Philosophers Group is in part dealing with mortality," Gib explains. "You don't have to be old to die. You could die today. Everybody needs to deal with the fact that life is temporary. When you face that fact, you can live fully." An especially rousing conversation explored what might lie beyond life, whether it's parallel universes or the Kingdom of Heaven. "That's where the discussion gets really interesting!"

The group also explores ways to make change in themselves and the world today. It encourages members to take tangible actions to promote positive change at whatever level is possible for them. The depth of intellectual discussion is certainly building a sense of community between Gib and his fellow philosophers. And, with ongoing work, he hopes they're playing a small part in raising the level of enlightenment at least in their group, and perhaps in the world around them.

TRY THIS

Do you have an off-the-beaten-track interest? See if others share your passion by searching your local Nextdoor or Meetup postings. You can also check community ed, the library, or local community colleges for classes and workshops. Once you've made connections, invite others to join you in regular meetings.

42
Zen of Photography
Susan, 65 years

Susan discovered quickly that one way to be happy in retirement is to develop a creative passion and "put some energy into learning it well." She put her energy into photography, investing in some good equipment and joining a local photography club.

The all-volunteer club offers classes, interest groups, speakers, and exhibits. Most importantly, it provides a community of people with a shared passion. "It's really helpful to be around people to guide you with your craft," says Susan. "And the more you get involved, the more friends you make. The club is definitely a source of new friends for me."

As a beginner, Susan relied on club members to learn how to shoot, edit, mat, and frame her work. Five years into retirement, she became the club president, helping new members with those skills and inviting them to participate in a new members exhibit at the studio. "I felt very proud of the twenty-four people in the exhibit," says Susan. "About fifteen of them were displaying their photos for the first time."

Susan's energy for helping others flows from her passion for the craft. "Photography feeds my soul. It takes you places into nature you might not go." For example, Susan learned of a pair of sandhill cranes nesting near her house one spring. She went daily to watch them sitting on their eggs and bumped into other club members enjoying the scene. "I saw the eggs as they hatched, just twenty feet away. It was so lovely," Susan recalls. "Without photography, that never would've happened."

Photography has a way of slowing you down. "I can be someone who's still under the influence of the to-do list," Susan explains. "I still feel the pressure to get things done." Finding peace with her camera is a real gift.

"When I go out with my camera and wander around taking pictures, I just follow the beauty," Susan says. "I get into the moment, and time stops. I want it to go on forever. It's very Zen-like."

TRY THIS

When do you lose track of time? Maybe it's creative pursuits like writing, sewing, or woodworking. Maybe it's practical activities like yardwork, home organizing, or walking in nature. Dedicate four hours to this activity. Notice how you feel. Explore how to build this into your life each week.

HEALING AND LOVE

43
Gentle Love and Healing
Mary, 67 years

Mary's brother Paul taught his children to believe that their Aunt Mary was going to hell because she's a lesbian. At annual family get-togethers Paul and Mary were polite and civil, but Paul's strong beliefs drove a sharp wedge between the siblings—until Paul was dying.

One December, Paul was diagnosed with advanced leukemia and given six months to live. His wife, Barbara, was soon completely overwhelmed with caring for her dying husband and their six children, including one son on the autism spectrum. When Mary called to ask if there was anything she could do to help, Barbara started crying and said, "Can you come?" With beautiful grace, Mary said yes. She had never been welcomed to their home before, but now they were all quietly willing to try coming together.

Mary joined Barbara at all of Paul's doctor's appointments, helping them navigate the complicated medical processes and prescriptions. At night, Mary slept in Paul's room to ensure that he didn't fall when he got up and Barbara could sleep without worry. For a precious passage of time, Mary gave gentle love to Paul, the brother who had been unable to accept her. The time was life-changing for Paul and his family, challenging them to grapple with how someone "bound for hell" could be filled with so much love and goodness.

Although Mary and Paul didn't have a formal conversation about forgiveness, slowly, very slowly, they began to heal their relationship. Mary explains, "Allowing me to be there with their family and letting me be useful in whatever way was helpful—that was our form of healing and acceptance." In his final days, Paul took Mary's hand and asked, "Mary, will you please take care of my family?" Their unspoken forgiveness of each other was transformative. It brought healing not only to the relationship between Mary, Paul, and his family, but to their parents and siblings as well. "My mother was *so* happy, my dad too. Mothers and fathers want this! They want their kids to be happy *together*," says Mary. "It wasn't that way for Paul and me. It's not that we fought. We just couldn't come together . . . until the end."

Today, Mary nurtures a special friendship with her nieces and nephews and stays in close contact with Barbara. She is profoundly grateful to have reconnected with her family again. She just wishes she didn't have to lose her brother to get there.

TRY THIS

Write an imaginary letter to someone you need to forgive. Express everything you feel about how their actions caused you pain. Then choose a peaceful space and ceremonially burn the letter. Silently say, "I let go of this pain. I forgive you." If you feel ready later, reconnect with the person you've forgiven.

44
In Sickness and in Health
William, 77 years

Williams and Shirley met at their church youth group in high school and fell madly in love. The young couple got married right out of high school, certain that their shared values, faith, and love would get them through life. When William's job moved them across the country and demanded sixteen-hour workdays, however, the strain on the young couple was too much. Faith and love alone couldn't save the marriage. "We loved each other, but our backgrounds were such that we weren't ready to handle difficulties," says William. "It was a different time then, when you just carried on. We both remarried and didn't interfere with each other's lives for years."

Forty years later, Shirley lost her second husband and saw the obituary announcing the passing of William's second wife. She reached out to William, hoping for reconciliation and friendship. They arranged visits to each other's cities and found themselves reunited by their shared faith. In slow stages, they started a process of healing. Just a few months into this renewed friendship, their faith was tested. Shirley fell in her garage and lay there for two and a half days before someone found her. When William heard the shocking news, he didn't think twice about helping Shirley.

William moved in with Shirley, pitching in to make meals, help with medicine, and handle the nitty-gritty nursing care of bathing and dressing. "It wasn't a rekindled romance or anything like that," notes William. It was just daily time together that allowed them to experience various stages of forgiveness. "I think there were so many layers of feelings and emotions to unravel. Explanations we never had. There was reconciliation," explains William. "We had a prayer life that really helped. It started with saying grace at meals. Then, as we talked about things, we'd put it into prayer. It became a daily thing, and we were grateful for that."

Despite this loving care, Shirley's health took a sudden turn that required several weeks in the hospital and time in a rehab center. William stayed with her through it all. After nearly a year of efforts to heal from her accident, Shirley passed away.

"I don't want to come across as some knight in shining armor," William stresses. "Helping Shirley just fell into place. It's just what I needed to do. And for a year I was able to care for her in the way you promise in your wedding vows. I call that a blessing."

TRY THIS

Does someone in your circle of family and friends need a little extra help? You don't have to move in! But you can offer to get groceries, provide a ride to a doctor's appointment, or help with yardwork. You can also check your local place of worship or nonprofit for people who could use some assistance.

45

Friendship and Love
Farah and Jen, 97 years and 56 years

When Jen and her family moved in next door eighteen years ago, Farah often chatted with Jen over the fence, admiring the young kids as they splashed in the plastic kiddie pool or made a sandbox volcano erupt with a garden hose. Other times as the family played, Farah quietly tended her garden between their houses, cultivating mint, onions, rhubarb, and gentle opinions about American parenting. Farah thought many American parents worked too much and spent too little time with their children compared to families where she grew up, in Iran. Each time the two women visited, Farah told Jen what a wonderful mother she was for being so engaged with her kids. Each time Farah complimented her parenting, Jen's eyes teared up because her own mother never offered praise. Slowly, Farah became a loving touchstone for Jen.

As the kids grew and the years gathered, the kiddie pool and sandbox made way for teenagers around a fire pit and loud backyard dance parties. During those years Farah's health took a challenging turn. First, she broke her neck in a terrible fall and endured a year of rehab. With a fierce will to live, Farah fought her way back to independent living, only to suffer a heart attack that required immediate open-heart surgery. Again, Farah wrangled her way back home, but now, at ninety-seven years old, she is too weak to go out like she used to. Still, the view from her kitchen window brings Farah happiness as noisy teenagers dance in Jen's backyard.

When Jen drops by to share a cup of tea, she marvels at how joy-filled Farah is despite her health challenges and physical limitations. Farah tells her, "At my age, what more can I ask for? I have my children who help with whatever I need, grandchildren who call, and you next door. So what more can I do? I can love . . . so I love."

TRY THIS

Our culture is so obsessed with doing *that we don't put much value on* being. *For ten minutes, practice being still. Sit quietly and just experience thinking about someone.*

PUT IT ALL TOGETHER

Would You Like to Take the Combo?

Those who flunk retirement were only interested in work. Get curious. Cultivate your interests.
—Bob, 84 years

There isn't one way to live a satisfying life. There are many, many ways.
—Gerry, 79 years

The majority of my interviewees combined several activities in order to engage their minds, move their bodies, and connect with others. The time they dedicated to each element shifted to match changes in their bodies, energy levels, and interests. No matter what, they kept finding ways to put it all together.

In answer to the question "What are you doing Monday morning?" every person I interviewed cultivated not one but several passions. At first, most had struggled to find meaning in this new phase of life. But through trial and error, with patience and curiosity, they found their way. When one activity was no longer interesting, they chose another. When I asked them what advice they would give to someone entering or feeling stuck in retirement, the most popular tip was to stay active and do good for others.

In response to "How do you want to move?" they typically dove into activities with both feet at the beginning of retirement, making up for neglecting fitness during their busy working years. As the years went on, each person sorted out the level and type of activity that kept them feeling healthy. Almost everyone made it a priority to move every day.

While figuring out "Who you gonna call?" they all faced challenges in dealing with family members or creating new friendships. But the longer the interviewees had lived, the more they emphasized the importance of nurturing your connections. Bob, at eighty-four, summed it up well: "You've got to take care of your relationships, or you'll be pretty lonesome."

The stories featured so far have been about single, standout activities. I highlighted individual examples to help you explore one possibility at a time and perhaps discover a match that inspires you. But most of the people I spoke with cultivated a collection of options. Although each choice, in and of itself, might not have been extraordinary, the combination of honoring mind, body, and relationships led all of them to age with joy and purpose. Let's see how people are putting it all together.

COMBINING MIND, BODY, AND RELATIONSHIPS

46
Cautionary Tales to Joy
David, 73 years

David got to share many of life's milestones with patients during his forty years in dentistry. He heard the joyful stories about births, graduations, and weddings, but he also witnessed the hard phases. "I had so many patients who were really great people," David says. "I saw them for thirty or forty years, and then in retirement they just stopped living. They changed completely." David made a commitment to never let that happen to himself. "I noticed the women didn't do too bad, but men really struggled in retirement. I'm going to do everything in my power to avoid that fate."

David also witnessed the impact on couples when one retires. He recalls, "One day I had a woman in my chair. The hygienist said, 'She's a little upset today.' I went into the room, and she started crying. I patted her hand and asked if everything was okay. She tearfully said, 'My husband is with me all the time. Since we retired he follows me everywhere. I can't get rid of him!' She was totally upset. I hear this type of story from men, too."

These cautionary tales inspired David to make a clear plan for his retirement that balanced his own interests with activities shared with his wife. To get started, he focused on all the things that he enjoys most. He works out at the health club on his own six days each week and golfs with his wife in a league. David values spirituality, so he makes time to meditate and read books on mindfulness. "This helps me be less judgmental. Less critical," he explains. He combines both priorities at the gym. After a vigorous workout, he takes a steam bath. "When I get in the steam it's nice and quiet. I cross my legs into the meditation position and do a short meditation, which is really good for me." David adds with a laugh, "I absolutely hate it when people come in and talk in the steam. It interrupts my Zen time."

Retirement also has allowed David to spend four months each winter near his daughter and granddaughters in St. Simons, Georgia. He and his wife got their own condo near his daughter, giving everyone enough space to be together and yet independent. They can pick the girls up from school and play or just hang out.

So far, the balance of activities in retirement feels just right. Nonetheless, David is open to change. For example, he's keeping his dental license current in case he wants to teach a class or do volunteer dental work. For now, though, David is "enjoying the heck out of retirement."

TRY THIS

If you have a significant other or roommate, start a conversation about how each of you envisions spending your time in retirement. How much time do you want to spend together? How much time do you need to be independent? Talking about your needs before there's irritation can help. Setting boundaries for time apart just might be the secret to wanting to spend more time together.

47
Cancer Inspired a New Path
Betty, 72 years

Getting tonsil cancer at age fifty-two motivated Betty to reevaluate her life. The health challenge grounded her in the knowledge that life's too short not to create the life you want. She felt even more motivated when her father began having memory issues in his midseventies. "I realized that if I get the same issues, I have just twenty-five years to use my skills," Betty explains. So, she got her finances in order and quit her job at age fifty-nine.

In the first year, Betty tried all kinds of volunteer opportunities. "I decided I wasn't committing to anything forever. I'd just do something for three months and see what happens," Betty said. "Many activities weren't satisfying, so I moved on." Thanks to dedicating time in her fifties to learning Spanish, she found her most engaging work in the Latino community.

Betty volunteered at Planned Parenthood in a Latina girls' program once each week. She pursued intensive training as an English as a Second Language teacher and taught classes twice a week for about five years. This built her language skills enough to let her run a volunteer resource center that helps Latinos solve daily challenges—her favorite role so far.

For thirteen years now, Betty has volunteered three days a week at the resource center which strives to decrease domestic abuse by reducing daily stress. Betty helps people handle critical issues, like finding jobs and navigating governmental processes. She also assists with simple, yet vital, roles such as sorting through mail. "People bring in bags of mail and need help understanding what's junk and what's important," says Betty. "They'll ask, 'How did they know I need a loan?' and I'll explain it's just a marketing letter. Other times I'll find a letter for a doctor's appointment that was last month. Then I help them reschedule it." One man came to see Betty five times to get help flying back to Ecuador to visit his parents. Betty helped him book the ticket and understand the documentation he needed to travel with his child, and when he called from the airport, she helped him figure out if he'd be charged for extra baggage. Tears rise in her eyes as she says, "Inspiring things happen every day."

In addition to her volunteer work, Betty does four to eight hours per week of paid contract work to make up for a bad market turn early in her retirement. Using skills from her former profession as an executive recruiter, she helps a small outplacement firm prepare clients for interviews. Laughing, she says, "In the morning I volunteer with dishwashers, and in the afternoon I work with executives. It's a funny mix, but I love it."

TRY THIS

Is there a skill you'd like to learn that could be your portal to new opportunities? Maybe it's a second language, a trade skill, or a teaching certification. You don't have to know exactly how you'll use it. Sometimes opportunities only show up when you're trained and ready to grab them.

48

Passions That Work with Your Changing Body
John, 68 years

J ohn believes you need to develop passions that can change with your needs in retirement. When he retired from teaching high school in Denver at fifty-seven, his first passions were golf, tennis, and other forms of exercise. But as his knees started acting up he realized, "My life can't be just a physical adventure"—a tough concept for a guy used to running multiple marathons.

He then consciously cultivated diverse interests that feed his mind and fill his spirit but are forgiving as his body ages. To engage his mind, John explores a vast range of hobbies and creative pursuits, such as taking a watercolor painting class, tying fishing lures, and making wine. (His wife thinks the wine still needs some work.)

One of his favorite activities is playing duplicate bridge at a happily cutthroat level of competition. John and his ninety-three-year-old partner are part of a league that runs intense, daylong tournaments with two hours of high-pressure play, a break for lunch and socializing, and then two more hours of games. John says, "There is no question that playing bridge is a conscious part of building my future. If my brain is working, I'll be able to carry this passion forward."

For his spirit, John devotes time to fixing things in his garage, viewing his "shop class" work as soul craft. He has always loved working on cars and currently is restoring a

VW bus. "Using my hands fulfills my spirit," John explains. He also nurtures his spirit by cultivating relationships. One of John's greatest passions is being part of a weekly men's discussion group, formed twenty-five years ago by two friends interested in connecting with other men. The men have free-flowing conversations about anything from politics to travel. "It's a very singular event that brings me joy. We don't socialize outside of the group, but we have a passion for each other. For example, when one of the members had brain surgery for a tumor, we were there to support him."

When asked what retirement advice he'd give to someone, he was clear: "If you don't have a hobby because you've been so committed to work, you need to be conscious—and I mean *be conscious*—about choosing three things you want to build a passion around that give you meaning. Be aware that when you retire there are things to be done that you may've ignored in life. It's now time to start focusing on the things that give you passion. Without doing that, I see people hitting the bottle too much. Traveling alone isn't the answer. Setting goals to create a beautiful day and then working to achieve it—that's the answer."

John is definitely following his own advice. The vast range of passions that he's cultivated will feed his mind, body, and spirit for many beautiful days ahead.

TRY THIS

Plan this next phase of life with the same care and excitement as you would a vacation. Ask yourself: What sights do I want to see? What do I want to learn about? How do I want to engage in this new place? Who do I want to travel with in my next chapter?

49

Pink Slip Leads to Joy and Connection
Claire, 60 years

A pink slip forced Claire into retirement. The number-one salesperson in the state for her company, she had enjoyed a thirty-five-year sales career and positive relationships with her managers. Her new boss was different. "Let's just say I was old enough to be his mom, and he found a way to get me fired," explains Claire. "But he picked on the wrong woman because it was so blatant how he got rid of me that I pursued legal action—and I won! It was unfortunate I had to seek legal action, but I had to do everything I could to resolve things."

Claire instantly began searching for another job. For a year and a half, she looked for sales opportunities, often making it to the final interview. Time and again, she didn't get the job. Then Claire tried jobs in nonprofits. That didn't work. She tried starting her own business. That didn't work, either. It was a brutal time for Claire, challenging her to question herself and wonder, "Who am I if I'm not a successful salesperson?" She had to face the reality of how much work had defined her, and she felt lost.

During this traumatic eighteen-month period, Claire endured other losses and challenges. Her daughter and only child graduated from college and moved far away to Chicago—a devastating change. Both of her parents died, amid complicated family dynamics. Her brother-in-law got cancer, and her mother-in-law encountered health issues. "I felt I was being attacked from all sides. Every aspect of my life was out of control." Claire sought help from a therapist to get through the dark time and leaned heavily on the support of her husband. With that help in place, she was ready to see this time from a new angle. "Some of us are a little more hardheaded than others," laughs Claire. "I finally thought, 'I guess God doesn't want me to work anymore. It's time to retire.'"

When we spoke, Claire was just six months into her retirement and happily shifting into a slower pace. "When I was working, my days and nights were so structured. Life was so hurried. I felt like I was always on a treadmill. I didn't realize how stressful it was until I stopped," she says. Now she consciously dedicates time to all the things she loves best: "I decided to create a clear vision for my retirement, and now I'm working to live that vision."

Claire works out six days each week to stay healthy. She found that it was best for her and her husband to work out at different times, to match their temperaments and give each other space. For time together, they are learning to play pickleball. They're clearly in it for the fun and friendship instead of the competition. On St. Patrick's Day they showed up to their league practice in glittering emerald-green hats, luck-of-the-Irish shirts, and sham-rock socks. "It's a *blast* and so much fun to do together."

Claire also volunteers for Random Acts of Flowers, a nonprofit that repurposes flowers from events to create new floral arrangements for people in the hospital or care facilities. "It's so fulfilling and touching," says Claire. "I never could've done this while working since it's all during the day."

By far her greatest joy is spending time with her grand-daughters, who live more than twelve hours away. When Claire was working, she and her husband could visit for just seven to ten days at a time. "The girls would ask, 'How much longer can you stay?!' It always felt like we were on a time clock until we had to leave again. Now we can spend the entire winter with the girls, and it's so, *so* great!"

Although Claire's retirement began with a jolt, she is now grateful for this new phase of life. "Now I get to live in the moment," Claire says. "I get so much joy from connecting with other people. Now that I'm off the treadmill, I can slow down and truly connect."

TRY THIS

If you didn't get to choose the timing of your retirement, grant yourself permission to grieve the loss of your past role. Reframe your newfound time as an opportunity to define the future you want to create. Start by choosing to do one small thing every day that brings you joy.

50

Get off Your Butt!
Stan M., 85 years

Although Stan was just seven years old when his dad died, he and his older brother started working to help their mother cover the bills. He remembers standing in the falling snow on a street corner downtown, selling shoelaces to passersby. "I think hardships like that and seeing my father's productive life taken away made me want to make every day count," Stan explains. "I think you're on this earth for just a limited time, and if the opportunities are there, why not partake in them? Plenty of them are free! Why not utilize that?" Throughout his life and into retirement, Stan has made the most of his time.

Stan stair-stepped into retirement, leaving full-time work as a pharmacy owner at age sixty-three and continuing as a part-time pharmacist at Target until age seventy-eight. During that time, he cultivated many hobbies and passions. He takes a weekly art class, has season tickets to the theater and orchestra, and sings in a choir that performs at senior centers and nursing homes.

Sports have always been part of Stan's life, so he walks or plays a racquet sport three times per week. He started with handball. As he aged, he moved to racquetball, squash, and then tennis. Due to injuries suffered in a car crash a year ago, he now wants to get into pickleball. Stan also enjoys sports as a spectator by attending many of his grandsons' hockey and soccer games.

Lifelong learning is also a priority for Stan. "I do online classes through edX, which sponsors free courses on subjects ranging from health issues to religion, economics to business," says Stan. "Currently, I'm learning about the pyramids in Giza." Over the past four years he has completed forty-eight classes. Additionally, Stan is learning to play the keyboard ("for my brain and fingers") and volunteers monthly for causes that he cares about.

Stan survived the loss of his first wife when she was only forty-nine (the same age as his father when he died). He remarried and lost his second wife fourteen years later. Today, he enjoys spending time with his longtime lady friend. In all of these relationships Stan says he "made it a point to keep learning, meeting new people, and socializing. All these things increase your knowledge, understanding, and enjoyment of life." When asked what advice he'd give to someone getting ready to retire, Stan smiles mischievously and says, "If the good Lord gives you the physical and mental ability to keep going, *get off your butt and do it!*"

TRY THIS

Sketch out an imaginary calendar, and list your favorite activities by day, week, and month. What will you include for your mind, for your relationships, and for your physical health?

CONCLUSION

Are You Ready to Choose Joy?

Take advantage of the opportunities that are right in front of you.
Some aren't that obvious, but if you look for the good stuff you'll
find it. —Gerry, 79 years

Are you ready to choose joy? Let's start today. Let's do it now! To create your "Plan to Choose Joy," focus on the three keys to investing your time in retirement. First, ask yourself, what are you doing Monday morning to engage your mind? What's going to give you a sense of purpose each week? Research tells us that two hours per week of purposeful activity improves your health.[7] Give yourself two hours *this week* to explore some "Try This" ideas from stories that nudged you to consider long-awaited dreams. Follow Joy's advice: "Do something to use your gifts, not just fill your time." Go ahead, give it a go! If one idea doesn't work, try a different one.

Next, decide how you want to move your body. If you have an established fitness routine, that's awesome! But if traditional exercise isn't your thing, choose three "Try This" activities to stay in motion. It doesn't have to be a huge time commitment. Just twenty to thirty minutes each day of any movement improves longevity and quality of

---

[7] Boyle et al., "Effect of Purpose in Life," 69.

life.[8] Bob M. said it well: "If you stop moving, you'll sludge up."

And finally, how do you want to connect with others? When you're feeling down or want to share something in your daily life, who you gonna call? Not Ghostbusters! If your friend list isn't what you want it to be, dare to do the hard work of connecting with others. Choose one of the many "Try This" options to begin forging new relationships. Staying connected to others is the biggest predictor of aging well.[9] Warren reminded us that "friendships and family dynamics aren't the most natural thing in the world. You have to work at them. Put your flaws out there and be open."

Now it's time to get out some paper or fire up your computer and write down which "Try This" activities you're ready to sample. If you'd like help developing your detailed "Plan to Choose Joy," take advantage of the free resources that go along with this book. Get your step-by-step guide at http://babsplunkett.com/choosejoy.

Think of my crabby grandma perched in the kitchen, wearing high heels and a scowl, and remember that you get to choose your attitude about aging. Make the most of your newfound time by investing your retirement with the three keys to aging well: engage your mind with purpose, move your body, and connect with the people you love. Start now. Choose joy!

---

[8] Lear et al., "The Effect of Physical Activity."
[9] Mineo, "Good Genes Are Nice, but Joy Is Better."